The Signifying Creator

The Signifying Creator

*Nontextual Sources of Meaning
in Ancient Judaism*

Michael D. Swartz

NEW YORK UNIVERSITY PRESS

New York and London

NEW YORK UNIVERSITY PRESS
New York and London
www.nyupress.org

Published with the support of Dr. Sigmund Stahl

References to Internet websites (URLs) were accurate at the time of writing.
Neither the author nor New York University Press is responsible for URLs
that may have expired or changed since the manuscript was prepared.

Library of Congress Cataloging-in-Publication Data
Swartz, Michael D.
The signifying creator : nontextual sources of meaning in ancient
Judaism / Michael D. Swartz.
p. cm.
Includes bibliographical references and index.
ISBN 978-0-8147-4093-4 (cl : alk. paper) — ISBN 978-0-8147-2378-4
(ebook) — ISBN 978-0-8147-0811-8 (ebook)
1. Jewish mythology. 2. Jewish legends. 3. Symbolism in rabbinical
literature. 4. Jewish art and symbolism. 5. Semiotics — Religious
aspects — Judaism. 6. Judaism — History — Post-exilic period, 586
B.C.-210 A.D. I. Title.
BM530.S88   2012
296.3 — dc23   2011043493
New York University Press books are printed on acid-free paper,
and their binding materials are chosen for strength and durability.
We strive to use environmentally responsible suppliers and materials
to the greatest extent possible in publishing our books.

Manufactured in the United States of America

10 9 8 7 6 5 4 3 2 1

For Amira and Sivan

Contents

Preface ix

Acknowledgments xi

1. Introduction: Outside the Text 1

2. Myths of Creation 13

3. The Semiotics of the Priestly Vestments 33

4. Divination and Its Discontents 55

5. Bubbling Blood and Rolling Bones 75

6. Conclusions: The Signifying Creator 91

Notes 95

Index 117

About the Author 120

Preface

The subject of meaning and how it is derived is not one to which I would naturally gravitate. As I imply in chapter 1, I have always been intrigued by the things that language does other than generate meaning. I have also spent a good deal of time analyzing language that most people think is meaningless, especially the language of early Jewish magic and mysticism. The inspiration for this work came during my study of the magical cultivation of memory and was further advanced while studying postbiblical concepts of sacrifice, when I noticed patterns of thought—expressed in midrash, synagogue poetry, and ritual practices—that I believe constitute a kind of indigenous semiotics of the nontextual.

I had been considering this idea while working on other projects when I was invited by the Skirball Department of Hebrew and Judaic Studies at New York University to give a series of lectures. They focused on bringing together some phenomena that I had observed while exploring some of the more unfamiliar corners of ancient Judaism, such as early Jewish mysticism and magic, the language and poetry of the ancient synagogue, and those sectors of Talmudic and midrashic literature dealing with such subjects as sacrifice, divination, and memory. This book, which emerged from those lectures, is not meant to be a comprehensive study of the idea of nontextual sources of meaning or of the individual subjects of these lectures. Rather, it is a series of vignettes. That is, the reader will not find an exhaustive analysis of rabbinic myths of creation or a catalog of divination texts and techniques from the Cairo Genizah. Likewise, although my argument is relevant to the idea, advanced in recent decades, that ancient Jewish thought constituted a kind of precursor to the modern critical theory of pantextuality, it does not engage the philosophical basis of that modern critical theory itself. Instead, I use these sources and methods selectively to illustrate a larger point, that ancient Jews looked not only to the text of the Torah and its textuality for signification but also to the world of objects, creatures, actions, and rituals, and that this tendency reflects a complex *mentalité* regarding how signification and interpretation are carried out.

Acknowledgments

This book is the result of many opportunities and influences for which I am grateful. First of all, I thank the Skirball Department of Hebrew and Judaic Studies for inviting me to inaugurate the Benita and Sigmund Stahl Lectures in Jewish Studies and Dr. Sigmund Stahl for endowing the series. At New York University, I learned many things, both specific and general, that I could not learn anywhere else; the influence of my teachers, including Baruch A. Levine and especially Lawrence H. Schiffman, should be apparent in these pages. I have also received much good advice from colleagues and friends at Ohio State University, including Professors Lindsay Jones, Sarah Isles Johnston, Fritz Graf, and Sam Meier, as well as Professors Ra'anan Boustan, Yuval Harari, Richard Kalmin, John Peacock, Peter Struck, Ilinca Tanaseanu-Doebler, Steven Wasserstrom, Elliot Wolfson, Joseph Yahalom, and New York University Press's anonymous reviewer. Jennifer Hammer of New York University Press guided this book to publication with unusual wisdom, acuity, and patience, particularly in the way she helped me transform these lectures into book form. My thanks also to Despina Papazoglou Gimbel and the edtiorial staff, and to Avram Shannon for his assistance with manuscript preparation.

An earlier version of chapter 3 first appeared as "The Semiotics of the Priestly Vestments in Jewish Tradition," in *Numen Supplements 93: Sacrifice in Religious Experience*, ed. Albert I. Baumgarten (Leiden: Brill, 2002), 57–80. Portions of chapter 4 appeared in "Divination and Its Discontents: Finding and Questioning Meaning in Ancient and Medieval Judaism," in *Prayer, Magic, and the Stars in the Ancient and Late Antique World*, ed. Scott Noegel and Brandon Wheeler (University Park: Pennsylvania State University Press, 2003), 155–66; and portions of chapter 5 appeared in "Bubbling Blood and Rolling Bones: Agency and Teleology in Rabbinic Myth," in *Antike Mythen: Medien, Transformationen und Konstruktionen*, ed. Christine Walde and Ueli Dill (Berlin: De Gruyter, 2009), 224–41.

My research and writing for this book were supported by grants from the College of Humanities, the Melton Center for Jewish Studies, and the

Department of Near Eastern Languages and Literatures at Ohio State University, and by a Fulbright-Hays Fellowship for study in Israel. Ohio State University's library—and especially its Judaica librarian, Joseph Galron—as well as the libraries of the Jewish Theological Seminary, the University of Pennsylvania Center for Advanced Judaic Studies, and the Jewish National Library and their personnel all have been enormously helpful in helping this book take shape.

Several months after these lectures were delivered, my father, Bernard Swartz, *zikhrono li-verakhah*, passed away. He was a lover of language, a voracious reader, and an excellent storyteller. My regret that he did not live to see this book in print is tempered by my gratitude that he was able to read and appreciate the texts of the original lectures. I also am grateful that I continue to learn from my mother, Marcella Swartz, my brother Steven Swartz, and especially my wife, Suzanne Silver. Their influence can be seen throughout this book, because they inspired me personally and because we discussed these subjects over the years. This book is dedicated to our children, Amira and Sivan. They, too, have inspired my work, not only as a source of pride, but through our lively conversations about words, music, art, and life.

1

Introduction

Outside the Text

Jews have been known for centuries as a "people of the book." This designation was first applied to Jews in Islam, which they have happily adopted as a description of themselves since the tenth century.[1] It is common to think of classical Judaism as the text-centered civilization par excellence, based on the Torah and its interpretation. But the culture of Jews living in Palestine and Babylonia in late antiquity, from the first century CE to the early Middle Ages, also carried with it a profound tendency to derive meaning from sources outside the text.

How and where people derive meaning is one of the most prominent questions in the humanities—indeed, some would say that it is the most important question in the academy. Much of what historians of religion do, however, is understanding the things that language does other than generate meaning. Current research on ritual language aims to find out not only what prayers, sacred poetry, and incantations say but also what they do. According to the classic formulation of philosopher J. L. Austin, we must understand both the informative function of language and its performative properties.[2] For example, the study of ancient magic and esoteric traditions, which has burgeoned in recent decades, analyzes language that most people think is meaningless. The student of magical texts must determine whether a given string of letters was a magical name composed of the initial letters of biblical verses, the mangled names of foreign deities, a phrase in an unfamiliar language, or perhaps just the language of the text spelled badly by an incompetent scribe.[3] When a solution does emerge—which is not always the case—the result is not always easily identifiable as the meaning of the passage. A particular phrase or combination of letters can be one of many ingredients in a recipe for getting something specific done, such as healing a headache, luring back an estranged wife, or expelling a neighbor from his house.

The argument of this book is that ancient Judaism encompassed the idea that God embedded signs in the world that could be read by human beings with the proper knowledge and consciousness and that this idea constitutes a kind of semiotics of the nontextual—that is, a form of discourse about the diverse functions of signs outside the realm of the written word. The next chapter discusses alternative creation myths, in which God is said to have implanted sources of signification in the Torah, the natural world, and the ritual system. The third chapter shows how rabbis and poets derived meaning from details in this ritual system such as the dazzling vestments worn by the high priest in the ancient Temple. The fourth chapter examines how ancient Jews developed systems of interpretation that read the divine will into everyday events and the intentional acts of animals and inanimate objects. The fifth chapter describes one of the ramifications of this latter idea, a conception of the world in which animals and elements of nature sometimes exercise agency in enacting the divine will in history. This book, therefore, is about how ancient people found meaning in unexpected ways.

The Significance of Meaning

The subject of this book, the significance of meaning, may be of interest to those who study language and culture for reasons other than the pursuit of meaning for its own sake. One reason is that some of the phenomena described in these pages, such as alternative creation myths and interpretations of the priestly vestments and divination traditions, take place in a ritual context. The first two themes are prominent in the poetry of the ancient synagogue, and divination traditions are complex ritual systems. Examining these themes thus opens the way to understanding their ritual function and their content.

Another reason is that these phenomena bear on how ancient societies formed theories and systematic conceptions of ritual and how that ritual is used to derive meaning. Ritual is an object of study and contemplation for modern students of religion, as well a subject of discourse for premodern cultures.[4] In the case of the alternative creation stories and interpretations of the priestly vestments, ritual is the main subject of interpretation, and divination is a ritual strategy for deriving signification. Thus understanding these topics can help us uncover indigenous ways of understanding ritual, culture, and signification: not only our own, modern theories, but also the theories that premodern societies themselves developed.

This inclusion of the study of how societies themselves speak about rituals and interpret them is indicative of a larger interest in what our informants and texts have to say about the nature of ritual action, hermeneutics, and historiography. The study of indigenous folklore theory and ancient ritual theory accordingly has become a growing field among anthropologists and historians of religion. For example, by studying the Pūrva Mīmāṃsā, the ancient school of the philosophical interpretation of Vedic ritual, Francis X. Clooney was able to develop a theory of how early Hinduism engaged in "thinking ritually" and to set Jaimini's commentaries into a conceptual framework comparing its insights with theories of sacrifice forged in the social sciences and cultural studies.[5]

A similar development took place in the field of semiotics, the study of communication focusing on the diverse functions of signs and their relationship to the signifier and interpretant. While anthropologists and linguists have long been engaged in applying semiotic analysis to the speech acts and material culture of non-Western and nonindustrial societies, only recently have they attempted to locate theories of signs, discourse, and historical events in those societies. E. Valentine Daniel's *Fluid Signs* does so from the perspective of the semiotic theories of philosopher Charles S. Peirce.[6] Richard Parmentier's *Sacred Remains* uses speech-act theory, which focuses on the active or performative properties of language, to locate indigenous historiography in Belau.[7] Such studies are not concerned with applying semiotic analysis from the outside to ancient documents or modern non-Western cultures but with exploring semiotic theories inherent in those sources and societies themselves.

To be sure, the discipline of semiotics has a long premodern history, going back at least to ancient Greece.[8] Likewise, the notion that there are indigenous semiotic systems in ancient Judaism is not new, as it can be traced to the nineteenth century. But the idea that semiotic systems in ancient Judaism embraced the physical world and active events is one that deserves greater consideration.

An interesting precedent to this argument can be found in a remarkable book, entitled *Doresh le-Ṣiyon*, or *Die Memnotechnik des Talmuds*.[9] The author, a nineteenth-century Moravian scholar named Jacob Brüll, describes how the rabbis tried to make the memorization of Talmudic traditions easier by means of phrases, acronyms, and word associations. This work is significant for the study of memory in rabbinic civilization, a subject that pertains to current debates about the oral basis of rabbinic literature and how it is used by historians.[10] But it is the introduction to Brüll's book that is most relevant to the subject of ancient Jewish concepts of signification.

Brüll introduces the topic by discussing the range of meanings of the Hebrew word *siman*, which means "sign" in its many varieties. This word appears first in rabbinic literature and stems from the Greek *semeion*, which also means sign.

The sign (*siman*) is unique in distinguishing between things that are similar, such as signs of cattle, wild animals, fowl, fish, and locusts, fowl eggs and fish eggs;[11] in distinguishing what is ritually pure from the impure; signs of a boy or girl who has reached the age of majority, a eunuch, or a barren woman.[12]

He begins his list of uses of the sign with anatomical features of animals or physiological features of the body, which are used to determine categories of ritual purity or dietary permissibility. Brüll continues: "People use them to make something known, such as a marking on a grave [which may be done on the intermediate days of a festival],[13] a vineyard in its fourth year, a fruit tree that is forbidden,[14] and a grave [the marking of which is specified in] M. Ma'aser Sheni 5:12." This next category of signs concerns the ways in which human beings place signs on objects or places in order to designate them as impure, forbidden, or permitted.

Brüll then discusses indicators of ritual time, such as when the stars come out, which indicates when evening prayers may be recited. Since this is a celestial indicator, he eventually moves to another category of sign making: the designation of certain events as omens, such as in 1 Samuel 14:9–10, when Jonathan, at war with the Philistines, waits for them to approach:

If they say to us, "Wait until we get to you," then we'll stay where we are, and not go up to them. But if they say, "Come up to us," then we will go up, for the Lord is delivering them into our hands. That shall be our sign.[15]

The idea here is that this event is a message from God about whether the battle will be successful. At this point Brüll turns to other examples of signs that God himself embeds in creation and in events. This category was crucial to the ancient rabbis, for they used it to distinguish permissible augury from forbidden acts of divination. Brüll thus moves from anatomical signs naturally embedded in animals and human beings, which are read and interpreted by people for ritual purposes, to signs that people themselves make to designate the legal status of a place or object, to signs placed in the cosmos, to those signs that God himself uses to send a message to humanity.

Brüll makes these observations in his introduction to a technical work about what were also called *simanim*, the mnemonic phrases and acronyms that Talmudic culture created to help in memorizing their complex scholastic traditions. That he places all these in this single category is worth noting.

In fact, his exercise in conceptualizing these categories as the term *siman* is not simply one of finding occurrences of this term, for some of the texts he cites employ the verb *ṣyn*, "to point or indicate."[16] What is remarkable, then, about this work is that in describing the diverse functions of signs and their relationship to the signifier and interpretant, this very traditional Moravian rabbi had stumbled on a kind of indigenous semiotics. Yet this book was published when Ferdinand de Saussure, the father of modern linguistics, was only seven years old.

After and Before Modernity

More recently, scholars of rabbinic literature and literary theory detected semiotic tendencies in rabbinic thought. One of the most prominent of these considerations is José Faur's *Golden Doves with Silver Dots*. Faur, who studies the Talmud and the medieval Sephardic commentarial tradition, sees in traditional rabbinic hermeneutics a semiotic approach to language and epistemology. He argues that the Greeks held a "metaphysical" view of the world in which the world is eternal and therefore "cannot signify," and he contrasts that worldview with what he characterizes as the "Hebrew," semiological view of the world: "The semiological view of the universe conceives of physical phenomena (and historical and personal events) as significant indexes that are to be interpreted and decoded as speech and writing. Therefore, the Hebrews reject the rigid 'nature/history' opposition. . . . Divine providence is to creation what *derasha* is to the Book."[17]

Faur further contends that this conception is not limited to how human beings read the divine word but to how God constructed the world from the beginning: "Through God the whole Universe is semiologically connected. God maintains a semiological relationship not only with man, but with all of Creation."[18]

Faur argues that in the first chapter of Genesis, God "calls" the things he creates in the first three days. But "within the cosmic semiological system, man stands alone not only in his power to refuse to respond to God's call, but also in his faculty to 'call upon the name of God,' that is, to initiate a dialogue with God." This, the semiological framing of the universe, makes for the mediation of communication between the divine and human realms. More than this, for Faur, this view of the world is inherently and entirely textual: "For the Hebrews meaning, signification, etc. are inseparable from text. Judaism does not recognize an a-textual problem: meaning is a function of text."[19]

Faur then seems to attribute to rabbinic thought a conception of pantextuality, the idea that all discourse exists within the realm of the textual. Faur was one of several scholars of rabbinic literature and literary critics who, in the 1970s and 1980s, saw in midrash and other rabbinic genres a kind of precursor to postmodern critical theories, from semiotics to deconstruction.[20] The idea of pantextuality is most commonly associated with the literary theorist Jacques Derrida, who famously declared that there was "nothing outside the text," according to his critique of logocentrism, the idea that truth resides beyond language.[21] Although Faur does not explicitly identify with Derrida's overall program,[22] other critics, such as Susan Handelman, sought to include Derrida and other poststructuralist critics in a stream that begins with the rabbinic hermeneutical tradition.[23] But as midrash scholar David Stern argued in 1996, some of those concepts, such as indeterminacy, have proved resistant to such identification.[24]

Faur's notion that the rabbinic conception of interpretation is a semiotic one is highly suggestive. It emphasizes the consciousness that the rabbis brought to their complex methods of interpretation. Especially valuable is his observation that in ancient Judaism, God relates through signs to humanity and all of creation. This argument will be borne out in this book.

At the same time, as critics have pointed out, Faur's argument assumes an overall opposition between Hebraic and Hellenic thought. Such a typology overlooks important historical nuances, not the least of which is the influence of Hellenism on rabbinic thought itself.[25] The rabbis first developed their religion, hermeneutics, and theology in a world dominated by Greek and Roman statecraft and culture, which abounded in institutions and practices based on the reading of signs in nature and biology, such as augury, haruspicy, and mantic professionals. These arts presupposed a world embedded with meaning. While skeptics like Cicero doubted the philosophical basis for these practices,[26] they were accepted by political leaders and the common people and also by Stoics and other philosophical schools. The highly developed semiotic theories of Greek and Roman philosophers and rhetoricians presupposed that textual and nontextual forms of signification were intertwined.[27]

As will be seen in chapter 4, Saul Lieberman, Michael Fishbane, and others have tracked the influence of ancient Near Eastern and Greco-Roman divinatory hermeneutics on the rabbis' textual hermeneutics. So too, philosophers, priests, and theurgists like Iamblichus saw in ritual and sacrificial procedures methods by which the gods revealed the ways in which the soul could commune with higher powers.[28] Even with the dominance of Christianity in the fourth century and after, Mediterranean culture and thought seems to have taken what Patricia Cox Miller calls a "material turn," in which objects, body parts, and images were seen to speak to the deepest needs of communities and individuals.[29] It will be shown here that this view of the world did indeed characterize sectors of Judaism in late antiquity. There is thus every reason to believe that these developments did not occur in Judaism in isolation from its cultural environment.

Moreover, the identification of semiological reading with pantextuality does not take into account the possibility that some semiological activities lay outside the realm of the text in the cultural and social environment inhabited by the rabbis. In other words, textuality may be a theoretical model that these critics subsequently attributed to all forms of interpretation, both textual and nontextual. To be sure, for the poststructural theorists who argue for pantextuality as an overall critical approach, this idea is inherent in all forms of interpretation; that is, the closed hermeneutical circle presumably would be operable at all times in all readings, including ancient ones. This argument, however, must be distinguished from the historical argument that this model of pantextuality was anticipated in Judaism of the rabbinic age. This book is not a refutation of the epistemological or philosophical basis of this argument; if it is relevant to this controversy, it bears on the historical argument that ancient Judaism constitutes an alternative to Western logocentrism in part because the entirety of its discourse takes place within the written text and its interpretation.

Theories of the Sign

In contrast, Jacob Brüll's earlier characterization of the role of signs in rabbinic thought is more inclusive. His introduction to *Doresh le-Ṣiyyon* invites us to see how the ancient Jews themselves saw the process of the creation of signs that in a religious conception allows human and God to communicate, both explicitly and obliquely. His essay unites the verbal semiotics of the oral Torah with the nontextual messages embedded, according to classical Jewish worldviews, in the earth, the stars, human actions, and such phenomena as the flight patterns of birds and the swaying of palm trees. Brüll's observations were originally meant to introduce the reader to Talmudic mnemonics, the techniques that the ancient rabbis used for memorizing their texts. His reason was that he distinguished among the sign vehicle, the object signified, and the interpretant[30] and thus placed in the same category the divinely created indicators of significance and human attempts to negotiate the text.

In doing so, he linked the physical designation of signs—such as the mark-ing of graves and the creation of cloven hooves—with the mental exercise of imprinting and recalling information.

Brüll's insights into the nature of signifying come into relief when we look at phenomena like ideas of sacrifice in postbiblical Judaism. Recent research on this subject shows that several poetic and rabbinic sources sustain a motif according to which God actively implanted sources of meaning in the world when he first created it. This idea appears in the legends of creation and redemption in Midrash, the classic rabbinic texts that interpret the Bible, and in the Avodah *piyyutim*, the elaborate synagogue poems that describe the sacrifice for Yom Kippur.[31] This motif is part of a larger worldview in which every thing created by God has a larger purpose in history. In fact, the idea that the things God created are not simply inert objects or dumb animals but actors in a drama of Israel's destiny extends to legends in which such substances and creatures as earth, blood, birds, and clothes have a will of their own. At the same time, according to this worldview, we humans have developed systems of interpretation and discipline in which we can uncover the hidden signifiers embedded in the physical world.

These sources are evidence that concrete objects, garments, and everyday events spoke to Jews in the ancient world no less eloquently and meaningfully than the Torah itself. The purpose of this book is to explore myths, systems of interpretation, and ritual strategies reflecting the idea that the physical world is embedded with meaning. Its argument proceeds in four stages. The first stage explores the idea that before God created the world, he created both the Torah and the Jewish ritual system and, furthermore, intended to signify to human beings by embedding meaning in animals, objects, and events. The second stage considers how one set of objects, the sacred vestments of the high priest commanded by God in the book of Exodus, served as the source of a large and complex system of interpretation in ancient Judaism, in which each detail in the high priest's garments is laden with meaning and at the same time serves as a ritual actor in the sacrificial system. The third stage exam-ines the ways in which ancient and medieval people developed systems for deciphering what they perceived to be hidden messages about human destiny embedded in everyday events and natural objects: techniques we call divina-tion. The fourth and final stage brings the topic back to creation and carries it forward to teleology by exploring legends in which elements of nature and created beings act out the divine will through their own agency.

This progression—from myths of creation, to interpretations of the priestly vestments, to divination traditions, to the actions of the signifiers themselves—also is a progression through the channels of communication between the divine and the human as perceived by ancient Jews. The myths of creation and destiny concern God's communication to humanity. In the priestly vestments, the communication runs both ways: God commands Israel to place signs of its identity and moral character on the clothing of the high priest, who then uses them as signifiers in his effort to secure atonement for his people. In divination traditions, human beings actively invent strategies for finding out the divine will. In stories of the agency of natural beings, the world itself not only communicates but also participates in history.

The title of this book is inspired by Henry Louis Gates's masterwork *The Signifying Monkey*, his exploration of types of subversive signification in African and African American cultures carried out by trickster figures and others. In one way, the sort of signification described here, in which God is seen to implant signs in the world that can be read in a variety of ways, could be seen as a hegemonic form of signification and therefore quite the opposite of Gates's subject. In another way, Gates does not exclude forms of authority in his study. He devotes an important section to how the gods in West African religions convey messages to humankind through the mediation of the trickster god (Esu), who in turn designates the linguist Legba to serve as interpreter.[32] Although Legba's methods are mercurial and can even be perverse, his function is pivotal in the institutional frameworks of divination, interpretation, and social structure.[33] In other words, to use Gates's terminology, this study concerns the act of "signifying"—conveying ranges of meaning and linguistic function from their divine sources through duly appointed forms of mediation—rather than "signifyin(g)"—subverting the conventional social order through misdirection.[34] Moreover, the system of semiotic mediation in ancient Judaism that is the subject of this book is itself an alternative to, if not a subversion of, the myth of centrality of the text of the Torah and its authoritative interpreters (sages or rabbis) that ostensibly lies at the heart of rabbinic Judaism.

The myths and methods of nontextual systems of meaning presented in this study may also turn out to represent social or cultural circles lying at the margins of rabbinic authority. Much of the evidence discussed here comes from rabbinic literature, especially Midrash, or rabbinic exegesis of scripture. The compilations of Midrash undertaken between the third and eighth centuries most likely represent diverse groups of rabbis and their colleagues, from the legal authorities that stand behind the early texts of *midrash halakhah* to the homilists and synagogue preachers that seem to have influenced and contributed to later midrashim. At the same time, this book draws on bodies of ancient Jewish literature, such as magical and divination texts and liturgical poetry or *piyyut*, that are not included in the rabbinic canon. While there is still debate about whether these forms of expression should be included in the category of "rabbinic" Judaism, it is clear that these literatures were not produced by the central shapers of the Talmuds.

This project has one more peculiarity. Although the subject is why nontextual sources were important to ancient Jews, the sources themselves are texts. That is, this book draws from the established texts of the rabbinic canon, such as the major midrashim and the compilations of biblical interpretation written in the fourth through eighth centuries, from synagogue poems written down in Palestine in the fourth through seventh centuries and available to us in manuscripts from the early Middle Ages and from manuals of divination from the Genizah and other manuscript collections, as well as the Talmuds. For the most part, this book does not encompass art history, even though the study of ancient Jewish art is currently undergoing an unprecedented revival.[35] Although a great deal can be learned from subjects like the function of art in the ancient synagogue, the use of drawings and physical objects in Jewish magic, and whether the Mishnah and synagogue poetry engage in the literary description of the visual, the main sources are texts describing the location of meaning in the physical world. The reason is that this book is concerned primarily with this idea rather than visual cultural expression per se. Thus, the very modest iconographic evidence for depictions of the priestly vestments from ancient synagogues is discussed in chapter 3, but only because they add to our other textual sources on interpretations of those vestments. In a similar way, Kalman Bland's book *The Artless Jew* argues that the stereotype of the Jews as a people devoid of artistic sensibilities is a modern invention. But because Bland's book studies the idea of the role of the visual in Jewish thought and not Jewish art itself, it does not include illustrations.[36]

Notwithstanding the irony of deriving the concept of nontextual sources of meaning from written texts, we must be aware that historians of religion often try to reconstruct rituals, social patterns, and worldviews from written documents. In the case of ancient Judaism, we are at least fortunate to have medieval and even ancient documents at our disposal, documents that tell us by their material context how they were used by the communities that preserved, buried, or discarded them. More to the point, the sources that explored here bear a complex relationship between textual and nontextual ways of knowing. Interpretations of the priestly vestments rely on scripture for their vivid imaginings of their physical beauty and meaning. Divination traditions often derive verbal messages from animals, events, and visual data and then write down their findings in manuals. Nonetheless, all these systems of signification see themselves as reaching outside the text and going directly to the world of objects and images for meaning.

This book is not the first attempt to challenge the notion that Judaism is exclusively a religion of the book. Not long ago, the Assyriologist Zvi Abusch detected a linguistic and conceptual relationship between the ancient Near Eastern process of oracular decision (Akkadian: *alaktu*) and the rabbinic legal process known as *halakhah*.[37] Several scholars have sought to locate the origins of ancient Jewish hermeneutics in Near Eastern divination and dream interpretation.[38] Howard Eilberg-Schwartz, a historian of Jewish ritual, entitled his collection of essays *People of the Body*, in which he argued that Judaic civilization is concerned no less with the human body than with the book.[39] This book builds on these and other explorations into the diversity of conceptions of signification among Jews in late antiquity. We begin by reexamining the theological underpinnings of these conceptions, found in ancient myths of creation.

Myths of Creation

According to the ancient rabbis, at twilight on the sixth day of creation God created the first pair of tongs. This detail appears in the tractate Avot of the Mishnah, known as the Sayings of the Fathers.[1] It is one of a list of ten things created at twilight on the sixth day of creation, a liminal time in prehistory. The rabbis' reasoning is as follows: A blacksmith needs a pair of tongs to grasp the iron to make another pair of tongs, and so on; therefore, the first pair must have been created by God himself.[2]

This statement is one detail among many in a rich tradition of myths of creation and precreation in rabbinic Judaism. The most famous of these is the idea that the Torah existed before creation. This chapter examines the relationship of this myth to alternatives, in which entities other than the Torah, especially the Temple, God's earthly sanctuary, were created before the world.

Myth in Judaism?

For generations scholars have recognized that ancient Judaism is rich in sacred stories reflecting the culture's worldview, a category known to historians of religion as *myth*.[3] But what does it mean to say that there is myth in Judaism? Historians of Midrash, the classical Jewish literature of biblical exegesis, and of Jewish mysticism have identified elements of myth in the literatures they study and have examined this question and its history.[4] Yehudah Liebes, following a pattern set by Gershom Scholem, the founder of the modern study of Jewish mysticism, defines myth as "a sacred story about the deity" and sees the history of Jewish thought from the rabbinic Judaism of late antiquity to the medieval Kabbalah as one in which conflicts between God and external forces are integrated increasingly into conceptions of God's inner life. For Michael Fishbane, however, the proliferation of mythological patterns in Midrash represents "the reverse process of domesticating original nature myths in the rabbinic framework."[5]

In these and earlier studies, the mythological element in Jewish lore is usually identified with creation. Fishbane, for example, argues that the Midrash allows the emergence of myths of God's struggle with the forces of chaos, represented by primordial monsters like the Leviathan as well as the personified sea.[6] In his study, Jeffrey L. Rubenstein, who shows how early medieval midrashic texts tend to express myths more directly than their late antique antecedents, takes an Eliadian view of myth. To him, myth "tells of the paradigmatic acts of the gods (God) or the ancestors."[7] Definitions of myth often expand the category to sacred stores that do not necessarily focus on origins. Most descriptions of myth also emphasize their use in the various contexts of performance, ritual, and social structure. Moreover, myths not only express the tellers' worldviews but also can reveal deeper structures of thought (*mentalité*) that underlie a culture's explicit stories and theories about the world in which it lives. Chapters 2 and 3 in this book focus on such a relationship among the making of myth, exegesis, and worldview in Judaism in late antiquity. We begin with a central myth in ancient Judaism and its alternatives.

The Blueprint for the World

One of the best-known myths of rabbinic Judaism is the idea that the Torah was created before the universe and was used as the blueprint for the world. There are alternatives to that myth, however, that can be found in Midrash and synagogue poetry. One of the principal alternatives, of equal antiquity and importance, is the idea that not only was the Torah created before the world but the Temple and the ritual system were as well. One significant idea emerging from that myth is that God implanted signs in the world to be read for the purpose of Temple worship and ritual observance.

The myth that the Torah was the blueprint for the world has its origins in ancient interpretations of chapter 8 of the book of Proverbs, in which Wisdom is personified as a woman, calling out to all men to abide with her and learn from her. At one point she proclaims that she was with God at the beginning of creation:

> The Lord created me at the beginning of His course,
> The first of His works of old.
> In the distant past I was fashioned,
> At the beginning, at the origin of earth. (Prov. 8:22–23)

Later on she says:

I was with Him as a confidant,
A source of delight every day. (Prov. 8:30)

In this speech, Wisdom seems to be saying that she was the first thing that God created—even before the physical world itself. From that point on, Wisdom coexisted with God. In verse 30, Wisdom describes herself as God's *amon*, a word that the Jewish Publication Society Tanakh translates as "confidant."

Since the rabbis equate Wisdom with Torah, they take this passage to mean that the Torah itself predated the creation of the world and, indeed, assisted in its creation. This argument for this idea is stated most elegantly in Genesis Rabbah, the major rabbinic commentary to Genesis, which was compiled in the early fifth century CE. The midrash takes as its starting point the meaning of the word *amon* in Proverbs 8:30, a subject on which the midrash registers several opinions. The text then attributes the following explanation to Rabbi Hoshaya:

> *Amon* [means] craftsman (*oman*). The Torah says: I was the handiwork of the Holy One, blessed be He. It is the custom of the world that when a king of flesh and blood builds a palace, he does not build it with his own knowledge, but with that of a craftsman. And the craftsman does not build it with his own knowledge, but from scrolls[8] and tablets that he has, so that he will know how to make rooms and furnishings. Thus the Holy One, blessed be He looked into the Torah and created the world. The Torah says "with 'beginning' (*be-reshit*) God created" (Gen. 1:1) and "beginning" means nothing other that Torah, as it is said, "The Lord created me at the beginning (*reshit*) of His course." (Prov. 8:22)[9]

The word *amon* can be revocalized to read *oman*, "craftsman." Furthermore, verse 22 of the same chapter states that God created wisdom "at the beginning of his way" (*reshit darko*). Genesis 1:1 begins *be-reshit*, which could mean "in the beginning." But the preposition *bet* could also be used instrumentally to mean "with beginning." Therefore, the midrash reasons, Proverbs 8 identifies Torah as the "beginning," according to which God created the world in Genesis 1. This remarkable idea presupposes a precreation as well as a hypostasized Torah actively involved in creation. It may also reflect a conception of divine wisdom akin to that of wisdom or *logos* in first-century Hellenistic Jewish thought. In the Wisdom of Solomon, extending and philosophizing the Proverbs tradition, divine wisdom is considered an "exhalation" and "effluence" from the power of God;[10] and for Philo of Alexandria, it is the Logos, the active agent of creation through divine reason.[11]

This idea has profound implications for rabbinic Judaism. If the Torah was the blueprint for the world, then, as the tractate Avot, the Sayings of the Fathers, says, one can "turn it over, for everything is in it."[12] It means that everything that human beings would want to know—cosmology, human nature, standards of behavior, the future—is contained in the Torah.

Precreation

Rabbinic literature does not confine the idea that God created something before the world to this one famous midrash. Both Genesis Rabbah and later midrashim contain several lists of things that were precreated, or at least preconceived, as well as lists of those things created at the very beginning of creation[13] or at the end of the six days of creation just before the Sabbath.[14]

There are several such lists, most of which share many of the same items, if in different order.[15] Lists are found in the following sources:

1. Sifre Deuteronomy Eqev, chap. 37[16]
2. Genesis Rabbah 1:4[17]
3. Tanḥuma Buber Naso 19[18]
4. Tanḥuma Naso 11[19]
5. Babylonian Talmud, b. *Pesaḥim* 54a
6. Babylonian Talmud, b. *Nedarim* 39b
7. Midrash to Psalms (*Midrash Tehillim*), chaps. 72:6, 90:12, and 93:3[20]
8. Midrash to Proverbs (*Midrah Mishle*), chap. 8[21]
9. *Pirqe de-Rabbi Eliezer*, chap. 3[22]
10. *Seder Eliahu Rabbah*, chap. 31[23]

Of the sources listed here, four—Sifre, Genesis Rabbah, and the two texts of Tanḥuma—belong to the classical Palestinian midrashim of the third to seventh centuries; Sifre Deuteronomy is one of the so-called Tannaitic midrashim, although the chapter under discussion may have been added a bit later;[24] Genesis Rabbah is dated to the fourth century; and the Tanḥuma is thought to have been compiled in the sixth or seventh centuries using earlier sources. The so-called Printed Tanḥuma (*Tanḥuma ha-Nidpas*) and the Buber edition are two editions of a text that existed in various forms in late antiquity and the Middle Ages.[25] The two lists from the Babylonian Talmud, which was redacted at the beginning of the sixth century, are identical, although they are set into different contexts: The list in b. Nedarim 39b is occasioned by a discussion of whether Gehinnom was created for the purpose of swallowing up Korah and his allies in Numbers 16, or whether it was precreated. The list in b. Pesaḥim 54a is preceded by list of ten things created at twilight on the sixth day and appears during a discussion about whether the fire of Gehinnom was created on the sixth day or before creation.

Most of these sources state that six or seven things were created (or planned) by God before the creation of the world. These are then listed, followed by biblical prooftexts that provide evidence for each item in the list. They vary in number and details, in the order of items on the list, and in their use of prooftexts. In fact, the passage in Tanḥuma, which is quoted later, has one set of variants: "Some say, also The Garden of Eden and Gehinnom." Sifre to Deuteronomy contains three items; Genesis Rabbah and *Seder Eliyahu Rabbah* list six. There are three lists in the Midrash to Psalms. In 90:12, one list of seven items includes the heavenly Temple, literally "the Temple of above" (*bet miqdash shel ma'alah*). The list in chapter 93:3 contains six items. The remaining sources have seven items. The following table summarizes these lists in the order given in the sources. Because the lists in Tanḥuma and the Babylonian Talmud have identical items and the same order, they are placed together here. Tanḥuma's citation of variants is noted in an extension to the table.

The earliest text, Sifre (usually dated to the third century), contains only three items. The next text, Genesis Rabbah, edited in the fourth century, has six. Only these two texts list the patriarchs (the "Fathers of the World"). When the Garden of Eden and Gehinnom appear together, Eden appears before Gehinnom in all lists except for *Seder Eliyahu Rabbah*, an ethically oriented homiletic midrash that makes a special point of emphasizing the punishment of the wicked. In fact, its version could be seen as a variant of Genesis Rabbah's, with the variant quoted by Tanḥuma substituting for the fathers and Israel. Unlike any of the other passages, the Midrash to Psalms 90:12, a commentary on Psalms 90:3, works the entire list into a comprehensive cosmological scheme in which the Torah is written at God's throne facing the heavenly Temple.[26] The midrashist then ties the homily to the next verse (Ps. 90:4) by arguing that according to that verse, since one of God's days is one thousand years in the sight of God, and the Torah was God's companion "day after day" (*yom yom*) according to Proverbs 8:30, the creation of these seven elements preceded the creation of the world by two thousand years. These last two sources reflect a development of the tradition in which the lists are integrated more thoroughly into the editors' homiletical program.

Lists of Things Created before the World according to Rabbinic Sources

Sifre	Genesis Rabbah[a]	Tanḥuma[b]	BT	PRE	Midrash Proverbs	Midrash Psalms 72:6	Midrash Psalms 90:12	Midrash Psalms 93:3	SER
Torah	Torah	Throne	Torah	Torah	Torah	Throne	Torah	Throne	Torah
Temple	Throne	Torah	Repentance	Gehinnom	Throne	Name of Messiah	Throne	"King Messiah"[c]	Gehinnom
Israel	Fathers	Temple	Eden	Eden	Temple	Torah	Garden of Eden	Torah	Eden
	Israel	Fathers	Gehinnom	Throne	Eden	Israel	Gehinnom	Israel	Throne
	Temple	Israel	Throne	Temple	Gehinnom	Eden and Gehinnom	Repentance	Temple	Name of Messiah
	Name of Messiah	Name of Messiah	Temple	Repentance	Repentance	Repentance	Celestial Temple	Repentance	Temple
		Repentance	Name of Messiah	Name of Messiah	Name of Messiah	Temple	Name of Messiah	Gehinnom	
		Variants							
		Eden							
		Gehinnom							

Note: BT = Babylonian Talmud (B. Pes. 54a and b. Ned. 39b); PRE = *Pirqe de Rabbi Eliezer* SER = *Seder Eliyau Rabbah*

a. In Genesis Rabbah, the Torah and Throne were precreated, and the other four items were conceived before creation in God's plan.

b. The lists in the printed Tanḥuma and Tanḥuma Buber are identical.

c. Heb. *Melekh ha-Mashiaḥ*.

In his dissertation, Yehoshua Granat conducted an extensive analysis of these sources as background to a study of the idea of precreation in the classical *piyyut* of the seventh and eighth centuries.[27] Granat distinguishes between the list of seven—including the Garden of Eden and Gehinnom, which appear first in the Babylonian Talmud,[28] and a Palestinian tradition beginning with the three entities listed in Sifre, which appear without enumeration—and the list of six in Genesis Rabbah and extending to the Tanhuma's list, which is similar to Genesis Rabbah's and in which the Garden of Eden and Gehinnom are listed as variants. He argues that the later midrashim, such as the Midrash to Psalms and *Seder Eliahu Rabbah*, reflect the influence of the Babylonian Talmud, which had become dominant after the rise of Islam.[29]

There also is a list of ten things that were conceived by God before creation. It appears in version B of *Avot de Rabbi Natan*, a commentary to the Mishnah tractate Avot composed perhaps in the third or fourth centuries:

Ten things were conceived before creation (*'alu ba-mahshavah*):
1. Jerusalem
2. The spirits (*ruhot*) of the Patriarchs
3. The light of the righteous
4. Gehinnom
5. The waters of the flood
6. The second (set of) tablets (of the Ten Commandments)
7. The Sabbath
8. The Temple
9. The ark
10. And the light of the world to come.[30]

This list contains only two items that appear in the lists in our table, the Temple and Gehinnom. This list of ten does not, therefore, appear to be related to that complex of sources.

For our purposes, however, most significant is that the Temple and Torah are the only two details that appear in all the related lists. The Throne of Glory and the name of the messiah appear in all lists but Sifre and the Midrash to Psalms 90:3, although that passage in the Midrash to Psalms lists the "King Messiah" himself. These lists are therefore evidence for an alternative to the myth of the precreated Torah, in which the ritual system—the Tabernacle or Temple, the system of dietary laws (*kashrut*), and other ritual requirements—was created or conceived before creation and serves as a model for future history. A closer look at some of these passages and related discussions shows how this idea has been explained and expanded.

The Primordial Sanctuary

We begin with Genesis Rabbah's version of the list, which contains many of the elements found in subsequent versions. Genesis Rabbah, however, distinguishes between those things that actually were created before the world and those that he conceived before creation:

I. Six things preceded the creation of the world. Some were created and some arose in His plan to be created.[31]

    A. The Torah and the Throne of Glory were created:

        1. The Torah, as it is written, "The Lord created me at the beginning of His course" (Prov. 8:22).

        2. The Throne of Glory, as it is written, "Your Throne stands firm from old" (Ps. 93:2).

    B. The patriarchs arose in God's plan.

        1. As it is written, "I saw Your fathers as the first fig to ripen on a fig tree" (Hosea 9:10).[32]

        2. Israel arose in God's plan, as it is written, "Remember the community You made Yours long ago" (Ps. 74:2).

        3. The Temple arose in God's plan as it is written, "O Throne of Glory exalted from old,[33] our sacred shrine" (Jer. 17:12).

        4. The name of the messiah arose in God's plan, as it is written, "his name endures before the sun" (Ps. 72:17).[34]

        5. R. Abahu be-R. Zeira said: Also repentance, as it is written, "before the mountains came into being" (Ps. 90:2), at that time, "You decreed, 'Return, you mortals'" (Ps. 90:3).

II. But I do not know which came first: the Torah before the Throne of Glory or the Throne of Glory before the Torah.

    A. R. Abba bar Kahana said: The Torah came before the Throne of Glory.

        1. For it is written, "The Lord created me at the beginning of His course, as the first of His works of old" (Prov. 8:22).

        2. This precedes that about which it is written, "Your Throne stands firm from old" (Ps. 93:2).[35]

The distinction between things created and things conceived in the mind of God seems to imply that not everything that appears on earth is a product of God's prior planning. As a consequence, when God places something in the earth by design, special attention must be paid to its existence and purpose. The phrase "arose in God's plan," applied, for example, to the patriarchs and thus signals that they were created in such a way as to fulfill a purpose in later history, a key feature of this motif.

Two things, the Torah and the Throne of Glory, were precreated; everything else in the list was conceived before creation and created according to that plan. Like Genesis Rabbah 1:1, this midrash mentions Proverbs 8:22 as proof that the Torah was created before the world. But it adds the Throne of Glory, God's celestial throne. The list of things that God conceived, to create later, begins with the patriarchs of Israel: Abraham, Isaac, and Jacob. The word in the prooftext from Hosea translated "first" here is *be-reshitah*, which the midrash associates with creation (*be-reshit*). Thus God "saw"— that is, conceived—the patriarchs in the beginning. At that point the midrash introduces the sanctuary or Temple, the abode of God on earth. This inclusion reflects a symmetry between the Throne of Glory, which is precreated, and the earthly Temple, which is preconceived in God's plan for creation.

This symmetry is as old as the idea of Torah itself. Several sources state that the creation of the Temple was not only preconceived but actually preceded the creation of the world. In the late third-century midrash Sifre to Deuteronomy, one passage seeks to prove that the land of Israel is more beautiful than any other land because it was created first. In the course of this argument, the midrash places the Temple along with Torah as two things created before anything else in the world:

I. So you find in the ways of God[36] that everything that is preferred precedes the other.
A. The Torah, because it is more beloved than anything else, was created before everything, as it is written, "The Lord created me at the beginning of His course, as the first of His works of old" (Prov. 8:22), and it says, "In the distant past I was fashioned, at the beginning, at the origin of the earth" (Prov. 8:23).
B. The sanctuary, because it was more beloved than anything else, was created before everything, as it is said, "O Throne of Glory exalted from old, our sacred shrine" (Jer. 17:12).

C. The land of Israel, because it was more beloved than anything else, was created before everything, as it is said, "He had not made earth and fields, or the world's first lumps of clay" (Prov. 8:26).[37]

This midrash begins at A, with the previous argument for the precreation of the Torah, based on Proverbs 8. But this passage then uses other verses to show that other entities also were created before all others. Thus in B, Jeremiah 17:12 is invoked to prove the primordial creation of the sanctuary. The verse speaks of the Throne of Glory as having been exalted from old— *marom me-rishon*—which can also mean "exalted from the first." The verse continues, *meqom miqdeshenu*, "the place of our sacred shrine," referring to the Temple. In C, the midrash shifts back to Proverbs 8. Verse 26 is used there to demonstrate the primacy of the land of Israel through the order of the terms for earth it uses. A gloss in the text of Sifre explains: "Earth (*ereṣ*) means all other countries; fields (*ḥoṣot*) means the wildernesses; and world (*tevel*) means the land of Israel."[38]

Just as the idea of a preexistent Torah can be derived from Proverbs, the idea that the tabernacle and Temple have a cosmic significance and a metaphysical reality beyond that of its role in the religion of Israel can be deduced from the text of the Torah itself. Scholars and exegetes, including Franz Rosenzweig, Umberto Cassutto, Moshe Weinfeld, and Jon Levenson, have pointed out that the Torah's narrative (in this case, the priestly source) describes the erection and completion of the tabernacle in Exodus 39–40 in parallel terms to its description of creation of the world in Genesis 1.[39] Moshe Weinfeld argues that this idea is reinforced by Psalms 132:8, in which God is called on to "arise to Your resting-place" (*menuḥatekha*), suggesting that the Sabbath's "rest" is the temporal equivalent of the Tabernacle as a resting place for God.[40]

The notion that the act of creation is mirrored in the building of the sanctuary follows from the idea that the Tabernacle was built on a kind of heavenly blueprint or prototype, a pattern (*tavnit*) that God showed to Moses on Mount Sinai (Exod. 25:9, 40). This in turn implies that the earthly Tabernacle and, by extension, the Temple, are based on the celestial abode of God and, at the same time, are a microcosm for the world in which the God causes his Presence to dwell (Isa. 6:3).[41] In postbiblical Judaism this idea developed into the concept of a heavenly sanctuary, in which angels hold sacrifices and sing God's praises.[42]

The Tanḥuma's version of the list of precreated entities makes explicit the relationship between this ancient idea and the rabbinic notion that the Temple and Tabernacle existed before creation: The following version is from the Buber edition cited earlier.[43]

I. Thus our rabbis taught: Seven things preceded [the creation of the] world: The Throne of Glory, The Torah, the Temple (*bet ha-miqdash*), the fathers of the world (and Israel); name of the Messiah; repentance; and some say, also The Garden of Eden and Gehinnom.

1. From [what verse] can the throne of glory be derived? As it is written, "Your throne stands firm from of old, from eternity you have existed" (Ps. 93:2).
2. From [what verse] can the Torah be derived? "The Lord created me at the beginning of His course, before His works of old" (Prov. 8:22).
3. From [what verse] can the Temple be derived? As it is written, "Throne of Glory exalted from of old, our sacred shrine" (Jer. 17:12).
4. From [what verse] can the fathers be derived? As it is written, "I found Israel as pleasing as grapes in the wilderness; I saw your fathers like the first fig to ripen on a fig tree" (Hosea 9:10).
5. From [what verse] can Israel be derived? As it is written, "Remember the community You made Yours long ago" (Ps. 74:2).
6. From [what verse] can the name of the messiah be derived? As it is written, "before the sun his name is established" (Ps. 72:17).
7. From [what verse] can repentance be derived? As it is written, "Before the mountains came into being" (Ps. 90:2); and it is written, "You return humanity to dust; You decreed, 'Return you mortals'" (Ps. 90:3).
8. From [what verse] can the Garden of Eden be derived? As it is written, "The Lord God planted a garden in Eden of old"[44] (Gen. 2:8).
9. From [what verse] can the Gehinnom be derived? As it is written, "Topheth has long been ready" (Isa. 30:33).

Having established that among those precreated entities, including the Torah, were the Throne of Glory and the Temple, the Midrash then goes on to elaborate on the relationship between the throne and the Temple:

I. Come and see:
   A. When the Holy One, blessed be He, said to Moses that he should tell Israel to make Him a tabernacle, [He] said to Moses, "Tell Israel that it is not because, as it were, I have no place to dwell that I tell you to build me a tabernacle."

B. Until the world was created a sanctuary was constructed on high, as it is written, "O Throne of Glory exalted from old, [our sacred shrine]" (Jer. 17:12); "and there a temple is built for My throne,"[45] as it is written, "The Lord is in His holy Temple" (Hab. 2:20); and so Isaiah said, "I saw my Lord seated on a high and lofty throne" (Isa. 6:1).

C. "But because of My love for You, I will leave My temple on high, which was established before the world was created, and I will descend and dwell among you," as it is said, "Make Me a sanctuary that I may dwell among them" (Exod. 25:8).

The midrash thus makes explicit the idea that the Temple is the earthly equivalent of God's heavenly abode but introduces the progression of history. That is, the heavenly throne of glory is God's abode until the tabernacle (and subsequently the Temple) is built, at which time God may dwell among Israel on earth.

Some sources take this idea even further and argue that the world was created for the sake of the Temple and the ritual system. This idea first appears in Genesis Rabbah 1:4, following the midrash discussed earlier, according to which the Torah was the blueprint for the world. Note the argument made by the midrash:

I. R. Huna said in the name of R. Mattenah: The world was created for the sake of three things: the dough-offering (*hallah*), tithes, and first-fruits,

A. As it is said, "In the beginning" (Gen. 1:1).

1. Beginning is the dough offering (*hallah*), as it is written, "the first yield of your baking" (Num. 15:20),

2. and "beginning" is the tithe, as it is written, "the first fruits of your new grain" (Deut 18:4);

3. also, "beginning" is tithe, as it is written, "the first fruits of your soil" (Exod. 23:19).[46]

This midrash sets forth in a remarkable way a ritual counterpart to the myth of the precreation of the Torah expressed in Genesis Rabbah 1:1. Just as that midrash associates the word *reshit* in Genesis 1:1 with *reshit* in Proverbs 8, this midrash links that word in Genesis 1 with its occurrence in three verses in which it refers to the first fruits, the first of the dough offered as *hallah*, and the first grains, which are tithed. Indeed, this midrash goes further than Genesis Rabbah 1:1 in stating that the world was created for the sake of those offerings.

The Avodah

The literature that most deeply reflects the idea that Israel's ritual system is embedded in creation itself is a form of synagogue poetry called the *Avodah piyyutim*. From late antiquity to the present day, these intricate, allusive poems have been sung in the synagogue on Yom Kippur, the Day of Atonement, as part of the service that recalls the high priest's sacrifice of purification and atonement in the Jerusalem Temple.[47] The classical Avodah piyyutim were written three to six centuries after that Temple was destroyed and are very important to helping us understand how ancient Jews understood such subjects as the nature of sacrifice, history, and the purpose of creation.

The poetry of the ancient synagogue is known as *piyyut*. Although it was often suppressed by generations of rabbis, its ornamental beauty and its deep exploration of sacred stories ensured its popularity for centuries. This literature produced dozens of poets and thousands of compositions before the rise of Islam. These poems were once sung in synagogues in Palestine during the classical age of the Talmuds and Midrash, from the fourth and seventh centuries. It could be argued that in fact, the discovery of this literature is second only in importance among Hebrew literary texts to that of the Dead Sea Scrolls for our understanding of ancient Judaism, for it preserves linguistic forms, myths, and ways of thinking that we would not have known about from Talmudic literature. This literature is also important because in it we hear the voices of individual authors. Although rabbinic literature is a collective literature, the first author of complete Hebrew texts after the first century CE whose name we know is that of the poet Yose ben Yose, whose work is one of the most important sources for this book.

The purpose of the Avodah piyyutim is to describe in great detail the Yom Kippur sacrifice in the Temple. One of the unique features of the poems is how they are structured. The Avodah consists of two sections. The first is an extensive introduction that begins with an epic narrative of the history of the world, from creation, and indeed before creation, to the election of the Jewish people, to the building of the Temple. The second section describes the high priest's sacrifice on Yom Kippur. This literary structure thus reinforces the notion that the Temple and the ritual system are prefigured by Israel's early history and, indeed, the history of the world. As a result, the poems express a teleological view of creation.

The most prominent Avodah piyyutim, Yose ben Yose's "Azkir Gevurot Elohah" ("Let Me Recount the Wonders of God") and another monumental, anonymous poem entitled "Az be-En Kol" ("When All Was Not"), work into their opening sections the myth that the Torah was the blueprint for creation. When speaking of the Torah, Yose ben Yose alludes to the tabernacle:

> At first, before a thousand generations
> it arose in his intention,
> and from it came the plan
> for all the works of the construction.[48]

The Hebrew word used in the last line, *tavnit*, translated here as "construction," refers to the creation of the world and also alludes to the prototype of the tabernacle shown to Moses in Exodus 25:9 and 40 and the blueprint for the Temple in 1 Chronicles 28:11. Here and in a fragmentary stanza in "Az be-En Kol," which is discussed in the next section, the poems refer to the idea that the earthly tabernacle that was to be built had a primordial supernal counterpart.

More than this, humankind was created for the purpose of praising God. In "Aromem la-'El," (Let Me Exalt God), a piyyut influenced by "Az be-En Kol" and "Azkir Gevurot," we read:

> This One[49] surveyed,
> and looked out at the world
> as a city without inhabitants,
> as an army without a commander.
> He considered this,
> and said, "What have I accomplished?
> I created and achieved, but who will recount My praises?"[50]

As Joseph Yahalom has shown, the idea that the creation of humankind has a cultic purpose is developed further, perhaps under the influence of our piyyutim, in Palestinian midrashim of the Amoraic period and later, from the fourth to eighth centuries. In chapter 6 of *Pirqe de-Rabbi Eliezer*, the great size and glorious appearance of Adam erroneously lead the creatures of the world to worship him. In response, Adam proposes: "Let us both go and clothe [God] in glory and might and enthrone the One who created us. For if there is no people to praise the King, will the King praise Himself?" This mythic idea, that God in fact needs to be created in order to be God, is stated most boldly in an earlier Palestinian midrashic source from the Tanḥuma-Yelamdenu literature published in 1966. The midrash is based on the word order of Genesis 1:1, which, following the usual order of subject and verb in biblical Hebrew, can be read literally as "in the beginning created God heaven and earth":

> "In the beginning God created" (Gen. 1:1). Fools say: "God created the beginning." But it is not so. Why? God said: "The owner of a ship is not called so unless he has a ship. Thus I cannot be called God unless I have created a world for Myself. Thus, "In the beginning created," and then, "God."[51]

That is, God could become God only through the fact of creation. Here, then, we can see the full development of an idea essential to the Avodah piyyutim, that the world and humankind were created for the sake of God's praise and that this function was essential to God's divinity.

For these poets, then, the Temple ritual is one of the fundamental elements of creation. For example, the piyyutim employ an idea found in rabbinic literature that the world was created from the foundation stone—the large rock in the Temple Mount now housed in the Dome of the Rock. This is reflected in a poetic allusion used often in the Avodah piyyutim. "Az be-En Kol" describes the high priest in this way:

> He began to perform (the sacrifice)
> of the lamb for the daily offering (Tamid)
> offering it entirely
> over that which is entirely beautiful.[52]

Here the poet alludes to Psalms 50:2, emphasizing not only the beauty of Zion but, according to a rabbinic exegesis of Psalms 50:2, that all of the world's beauty began with Zion.[53]

The Avodah piyyutim see creation as having been ordered teleologically so that each detail is created for a specific purpose in Israel's salvific history and ritual system. This pattern suits the purpose of the historical preamble, in which creation leads to the designation of Aaron and his performance of the Yom Kippur sacrifice.

The Creation of Signs

We have thus seen an alternative to the pantextual myth of creation, the idea that God used the Torah as the blueprint for the world. But how does this relate to the idea that God has embedded physical signs in the world for human beings to interpret? We turn again to the Avodah piyyutim.

Because the purpose of these poems is to recreate the Temple service, their literary structure reinforces the notion that the Temple ritual has its precedent in Israel's early history and, in fact, the history of the world. A long section in "Az be-En Kol" uses a literary pattern to indicate this idea. This section is an extended essay on the idea discussed earlier that the world was created by means of the Torah. Judging by the existing fragments of this section,[54] each stanza follows a specific poetic pattern. This section begins by describing how God used the Torah to create heaven and earth:

> Looking into (the Torah), You carved out
> the pillars of the heavens
> before there was primordial chaos[55]
> on which the rafters could rest.[56]

The next verse is fragmentary, but it expresses this idea in an interesting way:

> By[57] [its] weaving
> loops and twisted chains
> until you were to [——]
> to build Your Tent.[58]

As Yahalom points out, according to the Babylonian Talmud,[59] the clasps in the loops that held together the curtains of the tabernacle, according to Exodus 26:6, looked like stars in the sky. The poet then seems to be expressing the idea that the earthly tabernacle that was to be built had a primordial supernal counterpart. The section continues, enumerating the elements of nature that were created for the future. Some of these elements have an eschatological purpose. The poet speaks of God's creation of

> [——]
> Snow and smoke[60]
> until you kept them ready
> for the day of war and battle.[61]

Water was created with the flood in mind:

> With its compass you set a limit
> on the great springs of the deep

until they were to open
to blot out [all] existence in anger.[62]

and others were created for specific historical purposes narrated in the Bible:

With its pools you increased
fins and fowl
until You were to give commands
concerning a fish and a raven.[63]

That is, God created fish and foul with an eye to the days when he would command the great fish to swallow Jonah and the ravens to feed Elijah in 1 Kings 17.

These stanzas follow a specific pattern. The first line refers to an attribute of Torah, identified with wisdom, to which are attributed specific powers. The second line describes an act of creation, such as the separation of the waters and appearance of the land. The third and fourth lines are in the imperfect, implying either that God carried out that action subsequently in history or will carry it out in the future.

The stanzas follow the six days of creation. This form allows the poet to link two essential themes: the agency of the Torah in creation and the teleological nature of every created thing. Thus the waters are held back until they rise up in the flood; the ravens were created to feed Elijah; and so on.

More than this, God created animals for consumption and sacrifice. For example, in Yose ben Yose's "Azkir Gevurot," the creation of vegetation and animals is depicted as the creation of food:

There grew out of the earth
horned animals for slaughter
edible beasts,
both cattle and crawling things.

He pastured the Behemoth
with the produce of a thousand mountains,
for on the day when it is slaughtered,
He[64] will put His sword to it.[65]

The poem continues:

> The Creator exulted
> and rejoiced in His deeds,
> when He saw
> that his work was good:
>
> Grasses for rest,
> and food of choice;
> the table was set,
> but there was no one to relish it.
>
> He said to Himself,
> "Who will approach
> for the butchered animals
> and blended wine?"[66]

The purpose of the creation of humanity is the enjoyment of the food that God has created in both this world and the world to come, when the Leviathan and the behemoth will serve as meals for the righteous. It is at this point that the piyyutim articulate most clearly the idea that God embedded signs in the natural world. Yose ben Yose's poem "Atah Konanta 'Olam be-Rov Ḥesed" (You Established the World in Great Mercy)[67] explicitly connects, in the details of creation, the creation of food with God's intention:

> You made, as a sign, for those who know You[68]
> those who are clad with scales,[69]
> and a fleeing serpent[70]
> for the meal in eternity
>
> Did you not make out of the earth
> in great abundance
> cattle and crawling creatures
> and the beasts of the earth?[71]
>
> You set signs to be known
> of edibility for purity
> and for the company of the righteous
> you made the Behemoth fit to eat.[72]

And when the world was built,
in wisdom,
and when the table was set,
and its bounty,

You resolved[73]
to invite a guest
and to feed him
your choice food.[74]

Here, too, all creation is arranged for human consumption. That is, when God created animals, he was kind enough to place visible signs on their bodies so that Israel would know which of them were kosher, for both this world and the next. In describing God's creation of the animals, the poet uses the terms *tav*,[75] "mark," and *siman*,[76] "sign," to designate the anatomical indicators of the dietary laws (*kashrut*). They thus constitute a kind of teleological semiotics of animal biology. Likewise, in "Az be-Da'at Ḥaqar" (When He Surveyed with Knowledge), an anonymous piyyut in the tradition of Yose ben Yose,[77] the poet distinguishes between the animals permitted to the chosen people and those permitted to all others:

He placed signs of goodness[78]
for the people He chose
and all (animals), like the green grasses,
are for those He rejects.[79]

In Genesis 9:3, God specifically permits the eating of animals: "Every creature that lives shall be yours to eat. . . . You must not, however, eat flesh with its life-blood in it." God therefore gives edible animals to the nations of the world. But once the Jewish people stood at Sinai, God commanded them to distinguish between animals fit for consumption and all other animals. In order to make this possible, God therefore specifically communicated to the chosen people by means of anatomical indicators which were permitted and which were forbidden.

Torah, Creation, and Ritual

The purpose of this discussion of the preceding myths, midrashim, and poems is threefold: The first is to de-center the idea that the Torah was the instrument of creation and the main entity created before the world, by showing that in the minds of some ancient Jews, the Temple and the sacrificial and ritual system were thought also to be a primordial element of creation. The second purpose is to show that because of this alternative to the myth of the primordial Torah, the Temple, the sacrificial system, and the ritual system in general inspired creativity, poetry, and systems of interpretation. The third purpose is to explain that the ancient Jews believed that God embedded signification in the natural world so that human beings could use those signs in their daily lives. They therefore found meaning not only in their sacred texts but also in animals, events, and natural objects. The following chapters concern three consequences of these ideas: the surprisingly elaborate and complex systems of symbolism and interpretation that ancient Jews built around the garments of the high priest and his body; the art and science of divination, in which people develop systems of reading the natural world; and stories they told in which natural elements, objects, and creatures use their own sense of agency to carry out God's will.

The Semiotics of
the Priestly Vestments

Since the subject of this chapter is the significance of clothing, we begin with a kind of alternative fairy tale:

> Once upon a time, the emperor of a vast empire wanted to prepare for a great procession. He commissioned his best tailors, who made a great fuss of fitting him and flattering him on how splendid he looked. The day came and the great procession began. But all of a sudden, a child exclaimed, "But the emperor isn't wearing any clothes!"
> So the adults said to the child, "Silly child! Don't you know that clothes are a cultural construction anyway? Go home and read your Foucault!"

"The Emperor's New Clothes" is a story about what happens when a player in a ritual reveals the rules of the game. When we engage in rituals, we assume that no one will disrupt them by giving away the facts—that the bear we are hunting hasn't really agreed to be killed; that the football we are fighting over isn't really worth much; and that the piece of matzah we are eating isn't three thousand years old and wasn't really eaten by our ancestors.[1] This is what Catherine Bell, one of the leading theorists of ritual, following anthropologist Pierre Bourdieu, called the act of "strategic 'misrecognition' of the relationship of one's ends and means"[2] that is basic to how ritual works. When, for a variety of reasons, we start revealing the rules of the game, it is often because the ritual system itself has been called into question. It can be argued that this state of affairs, the result of what can be called a ritual crisis, gives way to discourse about ritual and its meaning.[3] One form that this discourse can take is the development of a system of interpretation in which every detail of a ritual or ritual object becomes a sign or symbol of something beyond itself. This chapter concerns one example of the ancient ritual discourse about clothing: the significance of the vestments in Jewish sources on sacrifice in the Hellenistic and Roman periods.

The previous chapter dealt with the idea that the ritual system, and the physical signs that accompany it, was embedded in God's primordial conception of creation. This chapter explores a consequence of this idea, that the vestments of the high priest form a key component of this ritual system and constitute a complex semiotic system that functions both instrumentally and expressively. To understand this idea, we must first consider the significance of clothes and their function.

Fashion, Antifashion, and Function

Dress is such a fundamental part of being human that we do not always recognize how complex it is. Clothing is both functional and deeply expressive. We obviously wear clothes for practical purposes, but we also are very conscious of what a particular garment says about the person who wears it, that person's place in society, his or her economic conditions, and even the ideology or theology to which that person subscribes. Because of this, dress is the subject of a great deal of discourse in human culture. In his classic essay *The Fashion System*, Roland Barthes lays down a basic principle for understanding the best-developed system of discourse about dress, "fashion":

> [A] Fashion Utterance involves at least two systems of information: a specifically linguistic system, which is a language (such as French or English), and a "vestimentary" system according to which the garment (*prints, accessories, a pleated skirt, a halter top*, etc.) signifies either the world (the races, springtime, maturity) or Fashion.[4]

Of course, the garments of the priest in the ancient Temple are the very opposite of fashion. The priestly vestments are presumably eternal and are meant for one person on earth at a time; only the high priest may wear them as he performs the sacrifice in the Temple. At the same time, they are worn every time that sacrifice is performed. They are ritual garments, and an important feature of ritual is its repeatability, in contrast to the presumed newness of fashion.

Yet Barthes has much to teach anyone interested in ancient discourse about the priestly vestments. We have the language of our sources—Hebrew and Greek as well as the exegetical, historical, and legal nuances carried by them—and a system of utterances about these ritual garments by which specific details—ostensibly opaque in themselves—can represent cosmic, mythic, or moral elements or the world of ritual behavior—such as the world of the patriarchs, Temple, or city cult—that such utterances are meant to evoke. More than this, understanding interpretations of the priestly vestments can also teach us much about how ancient Jews understood sacrifice, society, and communication between the divine and human. This is because clothes have the capacity to signal identity, convey power, and confer new properties on the wearer.

In fact, the analysis of clothing has one important sphere of affinity with the analysis of ritual. Students of the social roles of clothing stress that we can parse its function into instrumental, that is, active or performative, and representational, that is, symbolic or expressive purposes. For example, the instrumental function of a coat is to keep the wearer warm, and the representative function of the same coat is to signal the wearer's social status, youth or maturity (or aspirations to youth or maturity), and even his or her religious or political affiliation. Indeed, one can look to any highly factionalized religious environment, such as eighteenth-century Philadelphia or twenty-first-century Jerusalem, for some fine examples of the political nuances of coats and headgear. A system of discourse about clothing, such as fashion magazines, wraps around these functions a vocabulary imparting them immediacy and significance. Likewise, a system of discourse about ritual—be it Victor Turner, the sutra of Jaimini, Philo, or the Mishnah—creates criteria by which the material details of a procedure are meant to say more. The distinction between instrumental and representational notions of interpretation helps us understand ancient readings of these particular ritual garments.

To illustrate the potency of the vestments as indicators of status and cultic objects, we can look at how they served as a source of contention in Judea during Roman rule. According to Josephus, the first-century Jewish historian, the sacred garments were a subject of an ongoing custody battle between the Roman authorities and the priestly administration of the Temple. In his *Jewish Antiquities*,[5] Josephus tells us that the robe of the high priest was kept in the Antonia fortress, under state control, for safe keeping under Herod and was taken out, under an elaborate protocol, only for festivals and Yom Kippur. The Roman governor, Vitellius, returned them to the custody of the priests, but when Fadus later took them back, the Jews protested and the emperor, Claudius, feared that the protest would proliferate into rebellion.

In fact, the use of garments as markers of extraordinary beings in ritual contexts is an idea that can be traced to ancient Mesopotamia. As A. Leo

Oppenheim shows, in the ancient Near East, supernatural beings were said to be distinguished by their dress; that dress was in turn emulated by the priesthood.[6] As Oppenheim states, the use of gold and ornamentation by kings and priests "endowed these garments with the aura of sacredness which could not be transferred to other media."[7] Furthermore, over the centuries. this property of sacred vestments spread throughout the Mediterranean.[8] The elaborate garments of the biblical priesthood influenced Christianity in antiquity in both reaction and emulation. As Lynda L. Coon observes, although the simple clothing of Christ and his disciples

> inverts the ritualized garments of the consecrated Hebrew priesthood . . .
> [t]he late antique hierarchy . . . gradually transformed the simple, apostolic
> tunics of the gospels and Acts into a complex ritualistic assortment of vest-
> ments that physically embodied the unique powers (*charismata*) of Christian
> altar servants and through which masculine sacred gender was constructed.[9]

When the Temple was destroyed in 70 CE, the vestments, like all the accouterments of the cult, became of necessity not a physical object but an object of discourse only. In response to the loss of the cult, the rabbis continued to describe it and speculate about its regulations, yet held that the study of sacrifice was a worthy equivalent of the act itself. At the same time, the poets of the synagogue constructed elaborate recreations of the central annual sacrifice, the Avodah of the Day of Atonement, in which they tried to render the cult as vividly as possible.[10] An examination of how each of these groups interpreted the vestments offers us a model for understanding the changing attitudes of generations of Jews toward the sacrificial system.

The Components of the Priestly Vestments

The relationship between the active and expressive properties of clothing brings us back to our general theme, the semiotics of the nontextual in classical Judaism. The priestly vestments are also a special example of how communication between the realms of the divine and the human takes place through the implanting and encoding of signs. In Exodus chapters 28 and 39, God commands Moses, in the words of Exodus 28:2, to "make sacral vestments for your brother Aaron, for dignity and adornment." Moses is to instruct "those whom I have endowed with the gift of skill" to make them according to God's specifications. This is the first act of encoding, from God to Moses to the garment workers. At the same time, as we will see, the garments include precious stones with the names of the twelve tribes engraved on them, thereby encoding a representation of Israel to God. This is the second act of encoding. Finally, since both the physical objects and the verbal instructions for making them were present in the ancient Temple and written down in scripture, they were available for interpretation by the community of worshippers and sages. This is a third act of encoding—or, rather, an act of decoding. Note that all three levels of communication can include both the verbal and the visual, because the end result is a physical object determined by verbal instructions and eventually interpreted verbally. The signification thus works three ways— between God and Israel, between Israel and God, and between the vestments and the community that sees or reads about them.

The fundamental biblical sources for the vestments of the priesthood are Exodus chapters 28 and 39, from the priestly code (P) of the Pentateuch. Leviticus 8:6–9 also contains a brief narrative description.[11] The Mishnah classifies the vestments by distinguishing the four garments of the ordinary priests and the four additional components added to those of the high priest. M. *Yoma* 7:5 lists them in the following way:[12]

The High Priest serves in eight garments (Heb. *kelim*) and the common priest in four.
  1. a fringed linen tunic (*kutonet*);
  2. breeches (*mikhnasayim*);
  3. a royal headdress (*miṣnefet*);
  4. and a sash (*avnet*);

The High Priest adds to this:
  1. the breastpiece (*ḥoshen*, also known as breastpiece of judgment);
  2. the *ephod* (a richly ornamented garment);
  3. a robe (*me'il*, the hem of which was lined with cloth pomegranates and bells, apparently in an alternating pattern).
  4. The frontlet (*ṣiṣ*, also translated as diadem).

Here the Mishnah adds, referring to the divinitory instruments attested in Exodus 28:30 and elsewhere:

In these [garments] he would inquire of the Urim and Thumim.

The breastpiece contained twelve precious stones, the exact identity of which is still in doubt, engraved with the names of the twelve tribes. Two shoulder straps on the ephod contained stones, which are designated as "stones of remembrance of the children of Israel." In addition, according to Leviticus 16:4, the high priest changed from the golden garments of the daily service (the *Tamid*) to fine white garments (*bad*) when he entered the Holy of Holies once a year in his encounter with the Divine Presence.[13] Rabbinic classifications distinguished between those white garments and the gold garments worn during the rest of the year.[14]

More informally, the garments may be divided according to materials and functions:

1. Cloth garments for covering breeches, robe, tunic, and sash.
2. Headgear: *miṣnefet*, perhaps the diadem, and, according to Josephus and Ben Sira, a crown.[15]
3. Ornamental or cultic objects: The breastpiece and the precious stones, and perhaps the diadem, which functions more as a cultic object than headgear. The ephod may have fit into this category as well. Here can also be added the bells and pomegranates on the robe, which are the object of some speculation in interpretations.

These latter categories are not exact. It is unwise to distinguish too sharply between utilitarian objects, such as the robe, and ornamental objects, such as the breastpiece. All these garments had cultic value and were revered by interpreters for both their ritually instrumental and their symbolic properties. At the same time, the terms for some of these objects could be used for noncultic purposes and go back to secular functions. To give an example from rabbinic civilization, the term *avnet*, designating the sash worn by priests, is used in the Talmud and medieval sources also to designate an ordinary sash or belt worn by Jews.[16] Josephus uses both culturally specific terminology, such as the transliterated term *essén* for the *ḥoshen* or breastpiece, and common Greek terms, such as *chiton*, for the robe or *meʿil*. Nevertheless, most of the more ornamental objects, like the stones and the frontlet, serve as objects of special attention by interpreters.

There have been a few attempts, both in antiquity and modernity, to translate these details into visual form. In 1969 Moshe Levine constructed a model of the tabernacle according to rabbinic tradition, and especially Rashi, which was photographed and published by the Soncino Press.[17] Another imaginative depiction of the vestments appeared in Alfred Rubens's *History of Jewish Costume*.[18] Rubens based his depiction on Josephus's description, especially of the ephod. More recently, messianically oriented Jewish religious communities have produced graphic representations of the Temple and the vestments in conjunction with their general program of study of the sacrificial system in anticipation of the rebuilding of the Temple.[19]

We have two visual depictions of the vestments from ancient synagogues, but neither offers us a complete picture of how ancient Jews imagined the garments. The first is from the mural of the ancient synagogue in Dura-Europos on the Euphrates River in Syria, which was built in 245 CE. One of the panels of the synagogue painting depicts the consecration of the Tabernacle and the priests from Exodus, chapter 29. In that panel, Aaron is depicted standing in his full regalia. As Carl Kraeling pointed out in his original report on the synagogue, the artist rendered some of the details of the vestments, but not all, and had no access to either eyewitness accounts or Talmudic traditions. He evidently tried to render as many elements of the garments as he could, presenting them in the style appropriate to Persian nobility.[20]

The second is a tiny fragment from the recently discovered synagogue mosaic floor of the town of Sepphoris just south of Nazareth, built in the fifth century CE. This mosaic is a particularly rich example of Temple imagery.[21] Its panels depict a wide variety of images from Israel's myth and ritual, including the binding of Isaac, the zodiac, and especially the range of offerings in the Temple. Like the panel from the Dura painting, rows 3 and 4 of the upper portion of the mosaic apparently depict the ceremony of the consecration of Aaron in Exodus, chapter 29, and the daily sacrifice as described there and in Numbers 28. Although most of Aaron's figure has been destroyed, the remaining fragments show that the mosaic portrayed him decked out in his ritual garments, as described in Exodus 29. The small portion fragment of the garment that remains is bluish with yellow dots, a detail that also appears in the Dura painting. A bell on the hem of the robe also is visible.[22] The figure of Abraham at Mount Moriah is also mostly destroyed, although his shoes are off; this may reinforce the rabbinic assertion that the high priest officiated barefoot in the Temple.[23]

Both of these depictions were created after the Temple was destroyed. But when the Temple was standing, the vestments seem to have made a powerful impression on people who witnessed the sacrifices. In the Second Temple period, much effort went into describing this apparatus, particularly in Greek-Jewish sources. Josephus, Philo, the Letter of Aristeas, and Pseudo-Philo all describe it in lavish detail.[24] Josephus, in particular, adds many details that we would not have known otherwise and some details that emerge only later in the Avodah piyyutim.[25] Rabbinic literature contains a good deal of material on the subject, although it is difficult to gauge whether the amount of material is disproportionate in comparison to its interest in other subjects. The extensive excursuses on the vestments in the Avodah piyyutim deserve special attention because of their aesthetic properties and because they form a systematic statement.

Elements of Interpretation

Interpretations of the vestments fall into several motifs, some more pronounced in some sources than others:

1. There are stories of the miraculous origin and properties of the vestments. These appear in Midrash and in ancient Jewish magical and divinitory traditions.
2. One of the most widely attested motifs sees the priest as a symbol of Israel and its representative in the sacred realm.
3. Another, found mainly in Philo, Josephus, and the Wisdom of Solomon, sees in the priestly vestments a model of the cosmos.
4. A type of interpretation, found especially in late antique and early medieval sources, focuses on the active capacity of the garments to procure atonement or perform some metaphysical or material task.
5. There also are intriguing hints at a type of interpretation that sees in the vestments a conferring on the high priest aspects of divinity, or at least significations of divine authority.

The Miraculous Origin of the Vestments

Second Temple and rabbinic sources hint at the supernatural origin of the priestly vestments.[26] According to several midrashim, the priestly vestments were the very same garments that God had provided for Adam in Eden. C. T. R. Hayward argues that this idea may go back to the Second Temple era.[27] In Jubilees, Adam offers an incense offering immediately after he dons his garments.[28] Furthermore, Jerome and Syriac exegetes explicitly link the priestly vestments with Adam's garments, suggesting that they were familiar with the idea from earlier sources.[29]

This notion is fully developed in several rabbinic midrashim. In Genesis 3:21, following Adam and Eve's expulsion from the garden, God makes skin tunics (*kotnot 'or*) for them. The rabbis find in this phrase an occasion to make two wordplays. One is between the word for skin—*'or* with the letter *'ayin*—and light—*'or* with the letter *'aleph*. The second is the occurrence of the word *kotenot*, which is also used to describe the priest's tunic. Genesis Rabbah states:

> In the Torah of Rabbi Meir they found written robes of *light*. These were the garments of the first Adam that were like a lantern, wide at the bottom and narrow at the top. R. Revayah said: they were as smooth as a fingernail and as lovely as a jewel. R. Yohanan said: They were like the delicate linen garments that come from Bet She'an. Resh Lakish said: It was milk-white[30] and the first-born used to use it.[31]

According to this passage, Rabbi Meir's copy of the Torah read not robes of skin—*'or* with an *ayin*—but robes of light—*'or* with an *aleph*. The midrash then proceeds to explain what that means. All the interpretations take the phrase to refer to the appearance of the garments: according to the first interpretation they looked like a lantern, and according to the others they were bright and delicate. Resh Lakish adds that the firstborn of each family once used it to officiate as the family priest.

A slightly later compilation, the Buber edition of *Midrash Tanḥuma*, expands on this idea, although it does not mention the idea of the garment of light:[32]

I. How does Israel honor the Sabbath? With eating and drinking and clean clothes.
    A. For that is what the Holy One, Blessed Be He did: "And he made tunics of skin" (Gen. 3:21).
    B. What is a tunic (*ketonet*) of skin? High-Priestly garments that the Holy One, Blessed be He dressed [him in], as he was the first-born of the world.
    C. And further our Rabbis taught:[33] until the tabernacle was erected high-places[34] were permitted and sacrifice[35] (was performed by the first-born).[36]
        1. Therefore the Holy One, Blessed be He, dressed Adam in garments of the high priesthood, for he was the first-born of the world.
        2. Noah came and handed down to Shem, and Shem to Abraham and Abraham to Isaac and Isaac to Esau, who was the first-born.
        3. But Esau saw his wives practicing idolatry and gave it to his mother for safekeeping.
    D. Since Jacob took the birthright from Esau, it is only right that he should wear those garments: "and Rebecca took Esau's best garments that were with her in the house and put them on Jacob her younger son" (Gen. 27:15).[37]

This brief but complex tale weaves together several exegetical and literary motifs. The midrash belongs to the *tanḥuma-yelamdenu* genre, in which a question on a legal or ritual matter serves as an introduction to a discourse on a rather different subject. Thus the passage begins at I with a "legal" inquiry concerning how Israel honors the Sabbath. Although initially the question is answered by stating that Israel honors the Sabbath by wearing clean clothes, it soon becomes clear that the principal subject of the midrash is the origin of the garments of the patriarchal priesthood. The beginning and end points (A and C) are exegeses of two verses from Genesis that relate the garments mentioned in both scriptural verses to a single garment, a skin tunic, which is handed down from generation to generation. This tunic is identified as both Adam's first clothing and Esau's garment in which Rebecca dressed Jacob to deceive Isaac. That garment is none other than the primordial garment of the high priesthood of the pretabernacle family cult—the antecedent of Aaron's vestments. As the garment was passed down from father to son, Isaac was deceived not simply because Rebecca had disguised Jacob as Esau but also because Isaac would presume that Esau, not Jacob, would be wearing the ancestral vestment. The detail about Esau depositing it with his mother serves to explain why it was "with her in the house," according to Genesis 27:15.

The structure of the midrash is a folkloric and literary motif common to the Hellenistic world known as the *sorites*, or "chain of tradition," in which an object or tradition is passed down through a succession of ideal figures. This motif was first identified by Henry Fischel, who studied affinities between rabbinic and Greco-Roman rhetorical forms.[38] The most famous example of the sorites in rabbinic literature is the opening Mishnah of the tractate *Avot*, or Sayings of the Fathers, by which the Torah is transmitted from God to Moses through generations of disciples and eventually the rabbis. In this alternative sorites, the lineage is a priestly one, and the garment serves as the potent instrument of authority. Indeed, when Fischel first explored the idea of the sorites comparatively, his primary example from classical literature was Agamemnon's scepter in the Iliad (2.100–109), which was the signal of kingship deriving from the gods.[39] The primordial cloak functions in much the same way, acting as the authorizing agent by which the chief priesthood is conferred on each successive heir.[40] The midrash thus gives the vestment an instrumental role in validating the priesthood. More strikingly, it traces the origin of that instrument to God himself, who first made it for Adam, the firstborn of the world.

Another midrash reinforces the idea of the divine derivation of the priestly vestments by associating them with a miracle. In the tractate *Mekh-*

ilta de-Millu'im, an early rabbinic commentary to Leviticus, chapter 8, God himself is said to provide the priests with garments:[41]

I. "He put the tunic on him and girded him with the sash, clothed him with the robe, and put the ephod on him, girding him with the decorated band with which he tied it to him" (Lev. 8:7):

   A. This teaches that Moses was made assistant to Aaron. He would undress him and he would dress him.

II. And just as he was his assistant in life so was he his assistant at his death.

   A. As it is said: "Take Aaron and his son Eleazar and bring them to the mountain. Strip Aaron of his vestments and put them on his son Eleazar. There Aaron shall be gathered unto the dead" (Num 20:26).

   B. Whence do we derive that Moses did this? For it is written, "Moses did as the Lord had commanded. They ascended Mount Hor in the sight of the whole community. Moses stripped Aaron of his vestments." (Num 20:27–28).

   C. How could Moses strip Aaron of his garments in the correct order? Are not the outer garments always the outer garments and the undergarments always the undergarments?

      1. Rather, a miracle happened that God performed for Aaron at his death more than his life:

      2. Moses stood him on the rock and took off his priestly garments and the garments of the Shekhinah were worn under them.

   D. "And he put them on his son Eleazar" (ibid.). How could Moses dress Eleazar in the correct order?

      1. God bestowed a greater honor on Aaron at his death than in his life:

      2. For the garments of the Shekhinah were worn under. Moses went back and stripped Aaron of his garments in the correct order and dressed Eleazar in the correct order.

Lev. 8:7 depicts Moses as undressing Aaron and dressing him in his priestly garments. The midrash begins in I by showing that according to scripture, Moses officiated as the assistant (*segan*) to Aaron in his capacity as high priest. The passage then shifts in II to another instance in which Moses fulfills the same role, at Aaron's death, in Numbers 20:23–29. When Aaron was about to die, God commanded Moses to take off Aaron's garments and put them on his son Eleazar. The midrash asks in II C how he could put them on Eleazar in correct order, for if he did so he would have to take off Aaron's undergarments before dressing Eleazar, thus leaving him standing nude in front of God and everyone.[42] The answer, given in II C 1–2, is that a miracle took place. When Aaron took off his priestly garments, he was wearing "the garments of the *Shekhinah*" (the divine presence) under them. Thus God honored him "more in his death than in his life."

Other accounts of the miraculous qualities of the vestments focus on the stones of the shoulders and the breastpiece and the Urim and Thumim, said to be worn in the ephod. These often focus on their divinitory powers. According to Josephus, the stones on the shoulders flashed the appropriate message.[43] In the Middle Ages, these traditions are related to esoteric gemology.[44] Some traditions concerning those gems attested in the piyyut crop up again in medieval and Renaissance interpreters such as Baḥya ben Asher and Abraham Portaleone.[45]

Model of Cosmos: Philo and Josephus

One pattern of interpretation that seems to be characteristic of Jewish-Greek literature in the Second Temple era is the idea that the vestments are a model of the cosmos. Philo is the most celebrated and systematic advocate of that idea. For example, according to his *Life of Moses*,[46] the color and span of the robe create "an image of the air." The pomegranates and flowers on the robe represent earth and water, respectively, and the bells represent the harmony of the two. The ephod represents heaven, and the two stones represent either the hemispheres or the sun and the moon. The twelve stones on the breastpiece represent the signs of the zodiac. Josephus, who is somewhat more interested in describing the physical details of the vestments clearly, uses a very similar symbolic system, with a few variations in the particulars. C. T. R. Hayward suggested that for these interpreters, the Temple and its accouterments serve as a model of the cosmos. This idea is the centerpiece of Hayward's account of Second Temple notions of the Temple.[47]

A succinct representation of that view appears in the Wisdom of Solomon. In Numbers 17, by offering incense, Moses and Aaron avert God's intention to annihilate the Israelites after a rebellion. The Wisdom of Solomon describes the expiation as Aaron's action, achieved "not by bodily strength, nor by force of arms, but by word he subdued the chastiser, by recalling the oaths and covenants of the fathers" (18:22).[48] At that point it describes his vestments: "On his full-length robe there was a representation of the entire cosmos, and the glories of the fathers upon his four rows of carved stones, and your splendor on the diadem of his head" (18:24). The author has thus shifted our attention from a narrative that would seem to support an extreme instrumental view of ritual—that the incense itself as a material affects expiation—to a more purely representational view—that the priest represents the cosmos and Israel, and thus appeases God by persuasion.

Another type of allegorical interpretation relates details of the vestments to moral qualities. In his *Questions on Exodus,* Philo links the four rows of stones to the four virtues of knowledge, moderation, courage, and justice.[49] Naomi Cohen explained how Philo's terminology in these sections informs his moral language as well.[50] A moral interpretation of the meaning of the vestments also appears in the Testament of Levi, in which the patriarch is instructed to don the vestments: "And I saw seven men in white clothing who were saying to me, 'Arise, put on the vestments of the priesthood, the crown of righteousness, the oracle of understanding, the robe of truth, the breastplate of faith, the miter for the head, and the apron for prophetic power'" (8:1–2).[51] This variation on the purely expressive interpretation of the vestments provides an interesting contrast to Philo's. Whereas Philo's interpretation is allegorical, each row of stones *representing* a virtue, the Testament of Levi attributes to each vestment the *power* to impart a specific quality to the priest.

Representative of Israel: Rabbinic Literature

The mode of interpretation in which the priest wears a model of the cosmos seems to have been abandoned after the destruction of the Temple in 70 CE. In rabbinic literature, the most common system of interpretation of the vestments is the idea that the priest carries signifiers of Israel with him into the sanctuary. This notion is grounded in the Torah's statement that the stones on the high priest's shoulder straps are engraved with the names of the tribes: "And Aaron shall carry the names before the Lord on his two shoulders for remembrance" (Exod. 28:12). This verse makes explicit what is also implied by the placement of the names of the tribes on the stones of the breastpiece. Ben Sira also makes poetic use of this notion in his panegyric to Aaron:

> Precious stones with seal engravings
> in golden settings, the work of a jeweler
> To commemorate in incised letters
> each of the tribes of Israel. (45:11)[52]

In rabbinic literature, the idea of the priest as a representative of Israel is most clearly articulated in an exegetical essay on the significance of the basic elements of the costume that appears in the Palestinian Talmud, *Yoma* 7:3 (fol. 44b), in several Palestinian Midrashim, especially Leviticus Rabbah 10:6 and a Tanḥuma-like fragment published by Jacob Mann,[53] as well as, more extensively, in two places in the Babylonian Talmud.[54] These passages represent an interesting dialectic between representational and instrumental conceptions of the garments' function.

The exegetical occasion for the discussion differs among the texts. In the Talmuds, the occasion is the Mishnah's list of priestly garments mentioned earlier, and in Leviticus Rabbah, it is the preparation for the installation ceremony (*millu'im*) that Moses and Aaron perform in Leviticus 8. The Palestinian Talmud asks why the high priest serves in eight garments. The answer given by Hannaniah, associate of the rabbis,[55] is that the number eight corresponds to circumcision, which takes place after eight days. The text then quotes Malachi 2:5: "My covenant was with him [Levi]." The Babylonian Talmud makes clear that the exegetical occasion for the midrash is the proximity of Leviticus 7, which details various classes of sacrifices, to the discussion of Aaron's vestments in Leviticus 8:6–9: "R. Anani bar Sasson said: Why is the passage about the sacrifices placed next to the passage about the priestly vestments? To tell you that just as the sacrifices atone so do the vestments atone."[56] This conclusion is presented in the Palestinian Talmud and Midrashim as a separate statement independent of the exegetical question.

The focus of this passage is the power of the vestments to atone for Israel's sins. At this point, the midrashic pattern proper begins. The Palestinian Talmud's version is as follows:[57]

I. R. Simon said: Just as the sacrifices atone so do the garments atone.
II. "In the tunic, breeches, headdress and sash" [M. Yoma 7:5]:
   A. [The tunic would atone for those who wore mixed fabric (*kilayim*):[58] And there are those who said:]59 for those who shed blood, as it is said, [referring to Joseph's tunic (*ketonet passim*) in Gen. 37:31], "And they dipped the tunic in blood."
   B. The breeches would atone for incest, as it is said: "Make for them linen breeches to cover their private parts" (Exod. 28:42).
   C. The headdress would atone for the arrogant, as it is said: "And you shall place the headdress on top of his head" (Exod. 29:6).
   D. The sash would atone for [the thieves and, some say, for]60 the devious.

1. R. Levi said: It was 32 cubits long and he wound it this way and that.[61]
E. The breastpiece would atone for perverters of justice, and you shall make a breastpiece of judgment (Exod. 28:30).
F. The ephod would atone for idolaters, as it is said, "Without ephod and teraphim" (Hosea 3:4).[62]
G. The robe: R. Simon, in the name of R. Jonathan of Bet Guvrin, said: Two things were not atoned for and the Torah set a means of atonement for them, and they are these:
   1. One who speaks maliciously (*lashon ha-ra'*) and inadvertent manslaughter.
   2. For the one who says speaks maliciously, the Torah has set a means of atonement in the bells of the robe: "And they will be on Aaron when he serves and its voice will be heard" (Exod. 28:35): Let the voice [of the bells] atone for the voice [of the one who speaks maliciously].

At this point there is an excursus on the types of atonement for bloodshed. Finally:

H. Diadem: Some say blasphemers; some say the insolent.
   1. Those who say blasphemy can justly claim [that it derives from the verses]: "The stone struck [Goliath's] forehead" (1 Sam. 17:49) and the verse "on his forehead" (Exod. 28:38).
   2. Those who say insolence [derive it from the verse] "You have a harlot's brow" (Jer. 3:3).

The climax of the ceremony is the encounter between the priest and God. He thus, as we have seen, brings Israel in with him into the sanctuary. But if the stones of the ephod and breastpiece constitute a map of Israel on the body of the priest, the garments according to this interpretation present the deity with a map of Israel's sins. The purpose of the sacrifice, according to the garments, as it were, is atonement for moral transgressions. This is not a self-evident idea; it could be argued that purification of the cultic space is no less a function of the biblical Yom Kippur. Furthermore, the representational nature of the garments—that is, their ability to tell the history and constitution of the people—is at the same time their instrumentality. Each separate garment has a distinct role in the active effecting of atonement.

The Representational and the Instrumental in the Avodah

By far the most extensive and systematic consideration of the meaning of the priestly vestments in the rabbinic era is found in one of the most important sources for the study of sacrifice in postexilic Judaism. The Avodah piyyutim, which, in the process of recounting the Yom Kippur ceremony, dwell on the physical details of the sacrificial system, including the priestly vestments. Unlike the Mishnah, the Avodah piyyutim engage in an unusually elaborate glorification of the high priest.[63] Whereas the Mishnah is likely to depict the (Sadducean) priest of the Second Temple period as an ignoramus or heretic, the Avodah depicts him as pious and devoted. Moreover, the priest is himself an object of splendor. Based on a literal interpretation of Leviticus 21:10 that the priest must be "greater than his brothers" (*gadol me-'eḥav*), the poems depict him as exceptionally big and strong. As Yose ben Yose's "Azkir Gevurot" puts it,

> His strong body
> filled his tunic,
> doubled and woven[64]
> as far as the sleeves.[65]

It is in this context that we can understand the depiction of the priestly garments in these compositions. For example, "Az be-'En Kol" marvels how

> his stature
> rose to the height of a cedar
> when he was fit with embroidered garments
> to ornament his body.[66]

Both poems contain extensive descriptions of the vestments. These excursuses lavish detail on the exact design of the clothes, the breastpiece and the ephod, and the rings and cords that connect them. In fact, some of these details are found nowhere in rabbinic literature but are related by Josephus. This is a probably sign that the poets had access to independent priestly traditions. More important, the extravagant poetic descriptions of the priest's royal garments serve to make the magnificence of the ancient Temple vivid to listeners in the synagogue, bereft of the Temple.

The midrashic pattern that we have just seen, which seeks to demonstrate how each garment atones for specific sins, is also well represented in the piyyutim. Thus, following the description of the tunic just quoted, Yose ben Yose states:

> The sin of the house of Jacob
> was atoned by this—
> those who sold the righteous one[67]
> over a sleeved tunic.[68]

Here the poet has made more explicit what the Talmud implies, that Israel atones for its sins against Joseph when the priest's tunic—the antithesis of Joseph's blood-stained tunic—enters the Temple. Yose ben Yose also adds an original touch to the midrash that we have just seen equating the voice of the bells of the robe with the voice of malicious gossips:

> When [the bells] struck each other
> the voice of one with the other,
> they atoned for the voice
> of one who strikes his neighbor[69] in secret.[70]

"Az be'En Kol," an anonymous composition that, according to Yahalom, is earlier than Yose's, adds another dimension to this idea of the active role of the garments in expiation. The representative role of the vestments is articulated in a passage relating each of the gems on the breastpiece to one of the tribes as described in Jacob's blessing in Genesis 49. But according to this poet, it is the duty of the garments not just to represent Israel but also to arouse God's compassion for his people on the day of judgment and to dispel the malevolent forces. Thus he says of the bells:

> He set golden bells
> and wove them into his hem
> to recall [God's] love
> of [the one of whom it is said]: "How beautiful are your steps."
>   (Cant. 7:2)[71]

Here the word *pa'amon*, "bell," hints at the word *pe'amayikh*, "steps," in the Song of Songs. In fact, the idea behind this seems to be the rabbinic concept of "the merit of the fathers" (*zekhut avot*), according to which God is importuned to save Israel not because of its contemporary virtue but because of its ancestors' righteous deeds.[72] This is a common device in the rhetoric of prayer and is thus appropriate to the conventional function of Yom Kippur. Indeed, several centuries earlier, Ben Sira interpreted the bells in a similar way as arousing God's remembrance of his people:

> and a rustle of bells round about
> through whose pleasing sound at each step
> he would be heard in the sanctuary
> and the families of his people would be remembered. (45:9)[73]

But in "Az be-'En Kol," the vestments' active properties extend to their role in dispelling the hostile forces preventing purification. Returning to the bells on the robe, the poem makes it clear, following Exodus 29:35, that their function is both to atone and to announce, noisily, the presence of the priest to all present. As he steps into the sanctuary,

> When his soles moved
> they gave voice
> like him who called in the wilderness[74]
> to make a path straight.[75]

> The servants of the Divine Presence[76]
> were fearful of him
> for the robe was named
> after the One who wears justice.[77]

That is, the hostile angels in the sanctuary, who are essentially bodyguards fending off intruders in the sacred precinct, are frightened by the sound of the bells, which carry with it divine authorization. This notion is close to that found in the literature of early Jewish mysticism, which depicts the ascent of rabbis into the heavenly realm, in which they must ward off angelic guards using the authorization of esoteric divine names.[78]

The Priest as Representative of the Divine World

This function of the robe hints at another aspect of the vestments according to the Avodah piyyutim and a few midrashim: the idea that the priest is a representative of the divine world as well as of Israel. This motif can be traced back to Malachi 2:7, in which the priest is called a messenger, *mal'akh*, a word that can also mean angel.

An intriguing midrash plays on this dual nature of the priest. The midrash is based on an apparent contradiction in Leviticus 16. Verse 17 states that "no man shall be in the tent of meeting." But what about the priest himself? Leviticus Rabbah addresses this question:

I. "And no man shall be in the tent of meeting" (Lev. 16:17).
   A. R. Pinhas and R. Hilqiah, in the name of R. Abbahu: Even those [angels] about whom are written, "Their faces were the faces of men" [Ezek. 1:10] were not in the tent of meeting when he entered it.
   B. On the year in which Shimon the Just died, he said to them, "This year I [will] die."
      1. They said to him, "How do you know?"
      2. He said to them, "Every year an old man dressed in white and wrapped in white would go in with me and go out. This year he went in with me and did not go out with me."
   C. R. Abbahu said: And was not the High Priest a man? Rather, it is like what R. Pinhas said:
      1. When the Holy Spirit was resting on him, his face shone like torches. About him it is written: "The lips of the priest will preserve knowledge [for he is a messenger (*mal'akh*) of the lord of hosts]." (Mal. 2:7)[79]

Shimon knew who this man was because of his white clothes, like the linens of the priest himself.[80] The radiant appearance of the priest is also described in ecstatic terms in a popular hymn in Ben Sira 50:1–24, which found its way into the Yom Kippur liturgy as the piyyut "Emet Mah Nehedar," "Truly How Glorious":

> Like a tent stretched out among the dwellers on high
> was the appearance of the Priest;
> Like bolts of lightning going forth from the radiance of the Holy
>   Creatures
> was the appearance of the Priest[81]

The poem compares the appearance of the High Priest to heaven, the "tent" stretched over the angels as well as the flashing radiance of the Holy Creatures of Ezekiel 1. Yose's ben Yose's Avodah poem "Atah Konanta 'Olam me-Rosh" likewise describes the priest in heavenly terms:

> His likeness was like Tarshish,
> like the look of the firmament
> when he put on the blue robe,
> woven like a honeycomb. (line 103)[82]

Here we can hear echoes of Philo's use of the blue of the robe to represent the sublunar air. Lacking the specific physics of Philo, however, Yose clearly wishes his listener to think of heaven.

"Az be-'En Kol" describes the headdress in this way:

> Sparks of the seraphim
> recoiled from it
> for its image
> is like that of a helmet of redemption.
> . . .
>
> And[83] he placed on his forehead
> the frontlet, the holy diadem
> and his eyes
> shone like the heavens.
>
> And on it was written
> the letters of the Great Name
> "YY"[84] above
> and "Holy" below.
>
> And the supernal demigods
> made room for him
> lest their eyes be filled with [the sight of him]
> and grow dim.[85]

Here the last two themes we have seen are combined. The priest evokes the heavenly world so successfully that the creatures in the sanctuary make way for him as he enters. Thus he becomes a representative of both Israel and the divine world.

Conclusions

The systems of interpretation developed by thinkers and poets in the Second Temple and rabbinic eras had their origin in the nature of the vestments themselves. Visually striking yet mysterious, they called out for analysis as sources of signification and as ritual objects. Whereas all clothing signals information about such issues as the status of the wearer and his or her ideology and stance vis-à-vis society, the vestments gained additional layers of hermeneutical possibilities because their fabric, form, and order were commanded by God to be used in the ritual. At the same time, the vestments were presumed to have had an active role to play in representing Israel before its God. This led the way to a rich semiotic system in which each detail of the vestments could stand for something greater or perform a significant function in the ritual, depending on the interpreter's sensibilities. Philo, for example, granted the expressive function of the vestments a pedagogic role and a moral purpose as well, by maintaining that the priest, representing the world on his body, sought redemption for all nations.[86] Other Second Temple authors stressed the miraculous functions and the physical splendor of the vestments.

The need to develop criteria by which the community could understand the recondite details of Exodus 28 and 39 predated the loss of the Temple in 70, but those criteria were made more complicated by that loss. The rabbis sought to account for the reasons for God's laws by portraying the vestments as players in Israel's drama of atonement. The liturgical poets of the ancient synagogue, in contrast, presented the priest as both a representative of Israel and an active instrument in its entrance to the divine world. Their compositions thus reassured their audience that the sacrificial system was not only about morality and expiation but also the presence of God. Their descriptions of the vestments served this purpose by making the priest himself the vehicle of that encounter. It is interesting to think that by clothing the priest in a dense symbolism—of the cosmos, of Israel's sins and the merit of its fathers—the interpreters were in fact emptying him of his own personality. This reminds us of those schemes of sacrifice, such as that of Edmund Leach, that see the sacrificer entering a liminal world made up partly of heaven and partly of earth, bearing part of the community to the deity and part of the divine back with him.[87]

The poets and scholars we have studied here were, like ourselves, students of signification, which they found in the ritual garments. When the physical garments disappeared, they sought refuge in texts and in their memories of the high priest's visual splendor. Their discourse required self-consciousness to understand that ritual, like sacral clothing, was a system of communication whose channels could extend vertically, to the deity, or laterally, to the community. Their efforts to understand that system therefore found an appropriate focus in the dazzling, mysterious details of the high priest's vestments.

Divination and Its Discontents

In March 1982, Symphony Space in New York celebrated the seventieth birthday of the American composer John Cage by holding an event called "Wall-to-Wall Cage," a fourteen-hour marathon of composers and musicians performing his works and the works of others who admired and emulated him. Cage's works are well known for what are often called chance operations. One of his most famous pieces is entitled "4'33'," in which the performer sits at a piano and remains silent for four minutes and thirty-three seconds. In another piece, "Imaginary Landscape No. 4," the performer places twelve radios on the stage and tunes them to different stations all at the same time. The music then is whatever happens to be on the radios at that time. These pieces are not jokes or stunts; Cage wishes to focus the audience's attention on the ambient or random sounds that we ordinarily take for granted. Deeply influenced by Eastern philosophies, he wants the audience to cultivate a state of serene awareness of the implicit patterns of everyday sound.[1] Cage also used the *Yijing* (*I Ching*) as one of several tools to generate the data from which he designed his compositions.

During this celebration of Cage's birthday, a New York radio station interviewed Morton Feldman, another one of America's great composers and a man given to making oracular pronouncements in a distinctive Brooklyn accent. The interviewer asked Feldman about the role of chance in Cage's compositions. Feldman questioned the use of the term *chance* for describing what Cage was after. The following is a reconstruction of his comments:[2]

> I don't know about the word *chance*. We say we're taking a chance on love. But we don't say, we're going to have a baby, and we'll take a chance on whether it's a boy or a girl. You just have a baby, and—"Oh, it's a boy," or "Oh, it's a girl."

Feldman's point seems to have been that the joy in Cage's compositions came not from the randomness that results from the process he used to make those compositions but from how we allow ourselves to be receptive to those events or sounds that seem to be random.

If we are looking for complex systems of interpretation that rely on physical objects and events instead of texts, we can do no better than to look to divination, that ancient practice of telling the future or gaining information from seemingly random events, procedures, or patterns; from the shape of people's heads, to tossing dice or a bundle of sticks, or to gazing into a pool of water waiting for a vision. This chapter describes divination traditions in ancient and early medieval Judaism as well as how some of the ancient rabbis dealt with those traditions and some of the conceptions of the word and divine will that they imply.

These divinatory procedures rely on what we in the modern world call chance. But different generations and cultures have different approaches to the problem of chance. The idea of pure chance—that is, the idea that something simply happens without a purpose or intention behind it—is not an idea all societies share; indeed, the idea that everything happens for a reason is the premise behind the art of divination. Those conceptions of the world can be illuminated by highlighting some modern approaches to chance operations, how they differ with premodern approaches, and the problems they both share.

Dada and Divination

John Cage's attitude toward chance, as interpreted by Feldman, stands in contrast to the approach taken by an earlier generation of artists, the Dada and Surrealist movements of the early twentieth century. The Dadaists relied on chance operations for many of their iconoclastic works, for example, cutting up words from a magazine article and rearranging them randomly to produce a poem. These acts were an aggressive assertion of irrationality during the breakdown of the nineteenth-century moral and social order with World War I. Likewise, the Surrealists were interested in unleashing the irrationality of the unconscious but also took delight in random juxtapositions. "The situation of the surrealist object" was a principle whose motto was "as beautiful as the chance meeting of an umbrella and a sewing machine on an operating table."[3]

It is not as easy to generate irrationality as it might seem. Computer programmers know that the only way to generate random numbers, which are important to games and other programs, is by using complex algorithms. Since algorithms are, by definition, deterministic, the sequences they generate are called *pseudorandom*. A test of this randomness is how much repetition a procedure produces no less than how many unrelated choices result.[4]

Games, gambling, and other activities that depend on irrationality thus find several ways to produce it.[5] For example, physical ways of generating randomness rely on the fact that when we throw a stone or a stick, we cannot always determine where it will land. The human subconscious is probably the most obvious source of irrationality. We have access to the subconscious through dreams and hypnotic, hallucinatory, or trance states. This was the basis for Surrealism, and the Surrealist artist Salvador Dalí called his art "hand-painted dream photographs." Surrealist writers like André Breton used automatic writing, a technique by which the writer enters a waking dream state and writes down whatever emerges. Indeed, some of the most prominent Jewish mystics may have used such a technique.[6] As a result of a childhood illness, the artist Max Ernst had the ability to hallucinate by staring at a blank wall.[7]

In addition, our society regards children as a source of irrationality. Those who have romantic ideas of childhood think of children as being in touch with their inner, nonrational selves. But those who have less romantic images of childhood may think of them simply as not having developed the logical skills necessary to make rational choices. Of course, neither image is true; surviving in childhood is in many ways more difficult than surviving in adulthood, so as we will see, children make far more rational choices for their needs and environment than we think.

The generation of irrationality can also have another goal, one that may seem at odds with the access to the unconscious through dream states, automatic writing, and other ostensibly individualistic techniques pursued by the Surrealists and their contemporaries. For the Surrealists, the purpose of unleashing the unconscious was not to intensify meaning and individual expression, as it was for the Romantics, but to submerge them to impersonal forces. Writing in 1929, Walter Benjamin made the point that the automatism of the Surrealists functioned to blot out meaning rather than seek it out:

> Life only seemed worth living where the threshold between waking and sleeping was worn away in everyone as by the steps of multitudinous images flooding back and forth, language only seemed itself where, sound and image, image and sound interpenetrated with automatic precision and such felicity that no chink was left for the penny-in-the-slot called "meaning." Image and language take precedence.[8]

Likewise, Benjamin argued that the dream state pursued by the Surrealists had the effect of erasing individuality rather than accentuating it: "Language takes precedence. Not only before meaning. Also before the self. In the world's structure dream loosens individuality like a bad tooth."[9]

Benjamin's interpretation of the Surrealists' strategies brings out an important feature common to all three modernist practices, including that of Cage and his postwar colleagues: As much as they all relied on chance or the unconscious to break the cycle of causality and rational choice, they carried out their operations in highly controlled settings, which were designed to allow them to surrender their conscious will to an impersonal process. So, too, when someone throws a stone or a stick, the only given is gravity, which is likewise an impersonal force to which the practitioner can surrender. Looking to childhood as a source of inspiration also is to defer, at least putatively, to a mind not quite in control. At the same time, all these operations entail a ritualization of the artistic process through careful preparation of the environment.

This brief tour of the history of irrationality has brought into relief at least three approaches to the function and conceptual background of chance operations. The first, characteristic of Dada and Surrealism, seeks to release the modern mind from its presumption of causality by unleashing the unruly nature of both the subconscious and circumstance. The second, represented by Cage, seeks to promote a serene awareness of the sonic environment by breaking down the barriers between "music" and "noise." The third, represented by traditional systems of divination, seeks to uncover messages meant for humanity that have been implanted in objects, actions, and discourse by a willful universe or personalized higher power. At the same time, all three systems share some of the same challenges. For example, each system faces the problem of how to generate randomness effectively. Each also faces the need to efface the ego of the practitioner, albeit for different reasons.

The following survey of some forms of Jewish divination in antiquity pays attention to divinatory practices themselves and how they are presented in the texts in which they are found. In keeping with the theme of this study, this chapter emphasizes those sources whose meaning is derived from the natural world, especially signs and events that occur on earth, and those procedures for producing results of inquiry through active operations. Then stories and attestations to divination in Talmudic literature are contrasted with selected texts that give recipes and methods for practicing divination.

Divination and Interpretation

Divination may have been one of the first forms of hermeneutics.[10] From ancient Mesopotamia to Cicero, there is evidence that the roots of many of the hermeneutical strategies applied to texts can be traced to the ancient arts of divination. In his history of ancient theories of the sign, Giovanni Manetti sees Mesopotamian divinatory practices and Hellenistic theories of divination as precursors to semiotics.[11] Eric Leichtz sees the origins of scholarship in the Mediterranean and Western worlds in writings developed by Mesopotamian scribes struggling to preserve divination traditions through systems of classification.[12] Saul Lieberman and others also argue that the origin of some of the complex exegetical methods used in the Dead Sea Scrolls and in Midrash can be traced to divinatory procedures and dream interpretation.[13] This idea has both social and conceptual implications.

Divination, like other forms of hermeneutics, relies on a variety of social situations. "Everyday" divination can be simply a routine action that can be performed by anybody and does not require a special esoteric tradition to learn. We can think of games, such as those children play to guess whom they will marry, as examples. Other divinitory procedures are knit into the fabric of established institutions—the most obvious examples being temple oracles, military staff employed for war divination, and, in the case of ancient Israel, the Urim and Thumim, the oracles set into the breastpiece of the high priest in the ancient Temple.[14] That divination traditions can be one with textual traditions can be seen from extispicy texts from Mesopotamia, which are clay models of livers inscribed with instructions for interpreting their features and blemishes in order to predict the future.[15] In fact, fragments of such models were found in Hazor, in Israel.[16]

Still other divination traditions involve professionals or paraprofessionals who employ complex, technical, and usually esoteric methods for informing a client. Among these we can also distinguish two basic types. Some diviners work through a fairly technical procedure using manuals and secret lore, as well as a thorough inquiry of their clients, to tell the client's future and fate. The two best-known examples of this type of divination are astrology and dream divination. Each has deep roots in both Mesopotamian and Greco-Roman civilizations, and each has been used for both communities and individuals. A second type is the cultivation of a supernatural informing agent, like a spirit or angel, who then reveals the truth to the client through the diviner. The first type can be seen as a rough ancient analogue of the mechanical procedures for generating randomness carried out by the Dadaists and postwar composers, and the second type can be seen as a kind of precursor to the secular automatism of the Surrealists. Indeed, ancient Greek and Roman theorists of divination, such as Cicero and his interlocutors, distinguished between "divination by art" and "artless" divination—that is, those types of divination that employ technologies to interpret existing data and those in which a human being reveals the will of the divine through an internal process.[17] Even if those distinctions are not as tidy as ancient and modern thinkers have supposed,[18] they do alert us to the variety of social assumptions and technologies of praxis and transmission that divination entails. Yet because each form carries with it a different social valence, we must be careful about generalizing about divination and the degree to which it can be seen as socially disruptive—one criterion by which some historians of religion designate a given practice as magic.[19]

Divination also brings with it a variety of cosmological assumptions. Certain types of divination presuppose the intentionality of many things that are not living humans. Some types presuppose the knowledge and intentionality of animals, plants, and the like, as well as the assumption that they are concerned with the lives of entire nations or ordinary people. As Peter Struck points out, Cicero raises such issues in his *De divinatione*, by placing an explanation in the mouth of his brother Quintus of how minute details like entrails and bird songs can indicate the divine will:

> The gods are not directly responsible for every fissure in the liver or for every song of a bird, since, manifestly, that would not be seemly or proper in a god and furthermore is impossible. But, in the beginning, the universe was so created that certain results would be preceded by certain signs, which are given sometimes by entrails and by birds, sometimes by lightning, by portents, and by stars, sometimes by dreams, and sometimes by utterances of persons in a frenzy. . . . Assuming the proposition to be conceded that there is a divine power which pervades the lives of men, it is not hard to understand the principle directing those premonitory signs which we see come to pass.[20]

That is, the gods embedded signs and messages into the universe, not necessarily by individual intent, but by the very structure of creation. In this and the next chapter, we explore how a variant of this idea is expressed in ancient Jewish thought.

Likewise, necromancy—that is, the consultation of the dead—an idea that survives into modern culture, from séances to television detective shows, presupposes that the dead know things that we do not—an assumption that should not be seen as self-evident. Quintus's theory of how dreams can foretell the future is relevant to this problem:

> Such is the rationale of prophecy by means of frenzy, and that of dreams is not much unlike it. For the revelations made to seers when awake are made to us in sleep. While we sleep and the body lies as if dead, the soul is at its best, because it is then freed from the influence of the physical senses and from the worldly cares that weigh it down. And since the soul has lived from all eternity and has had converse with numberless other souls, it sees everything that exists in nature, provided that moderation and restraint have been used in eating and in drinking, so that the soul is in a condition to watch while the body sleeps. Such is the explanation of divination by dreams.[21]

That is, the dead soul, unmoored from its former body, has a chance during sleep to converse with other souls who are informed about what is happening in their local environments. This theory also hints at an answer to the question of how it is that the dead know something we do not. Free-floating souls can converse with one another about the affairs of the world in a way that we, anchored to the earth, cannot.

Cicero used Quintus as a spokesman for Stoic theories of divination, which are then refuted by Cicero's skepticism. Both Quintus's theory of divination and Cicero's suspicions were conditioned by their philosophical background. Ancient Jews likewise practiced forms of divination that were very similar to those of their Mediterranean neighbors. At the same time, those forms, as well as the discourse about them carried out by religious professionals, reveal a good deal about how ancient Jewish culture understood divinatory revelation and its underlying realities.

The Roots of Divination

Jewish divination has a long and distinguished history.[22] On the face of it, certain types of divination seem to be prohibited by the Torah. Leviticus 19:26 states lo tenahashu ve-lo te'onenu, rendered by the New Jewish Publication Society (NJPS) translation as "you shall not practice divination or soothsaying." But exactly what actions these words refer to is not clear.[23] Moreover, a system of oracles is built into the ritual system, the mysterious Urim and Thumim on the breastpiece of the high priest, and other instances of divinatory practices sanctioned by biblical authors.[24]

Divination texts themselves go back to the Dead Sea Scrolls, in which at least two types of divination are attested. An example is 4Q318, an astrological text that includes the practice of brontology, or the prediction of the future by means of telling what will happen if it thunders during a particular sign in the zodiac:

> If it thunders [in (the sign of) Taurus,] revolutions against [. . .] [and] affliction for the province and a swo[rd in the cour]t of the King and in the province[. . .] there will be. And for the Arabs, [. . .] famine. And they will plunder each oth[er.] If it thunders in [the sign of Gemini], fear and distress from the foreigners and [. . .][25]

One of the many interesting things about this cryptic text is that its predictions are valid not for individuals but for the nation as a whole. This reminds us that for ancient peoples—from Mesopotamian civilizations to ancient Rome—divination was inseparable from statecraft, and diviners were part of the empire's political structure. The social nature of this text's predictions is also in keeping with the collectivism of the Dead Sea community, which may not have written this text but did preserve it. Likewise, other Qumran texts may indicate that physical features of individuals qualified them for a certain status in the sect. In fact, there may be links between the physiognomic literature at Qumran and those from esoteric circles in late antiquity and the early Middle Ages. Physiognomy seems to have played a part in determining where an individual member of the sect stood according to the doctrine of the Two Spirits, by which every person was said to possess the positive or negative essence that qualified or disqualified him or her for membership in the sect.[26] These documents therefore point in several directions: outward, to the social system at Qumran, back in time to Mesopotamian divinitory traditions, and forward to the physiognomic texts related to early Jewish mystical literature.

Sources of Divination

The Cairo Genizah preserved many texts that can be directly traced to Palestine in the first few centuries of the Common Era. One such source is a recently published lunar omen text in Palestinian Aramaic.[27] The text is an Aramaic rhyme composed for the sanctification of the new moon at Nisan. This text, perhaps with an eye to its liturgical function, emphasizes information of interest to the nation:

If the moon is . . . like snow in the month of Elul, you should know that it [the land] will be smitten with snow. There will be a great dissension in the world between Israel and the government. The moon is never eclipsed in Tishri. But if it is eclipsed, it is a bad sign for the "enemies of the Jews."[28] Religious persecution will issue from the kingdom and woeful destruction will be upon the Jews.[29]

Astrology and related forms of divination based on celestial events are thus well attested in ancient and medieval Judaism.[30] At least two texts written in Greek, preserved in Syriac, and of apparent Jewish provenance, perhaps from the first century BCE or CE, take the form of pseudepigraphic astrological manuals.[31] Hebrew names of zodiac signs are scattered throughout rabbinic literature; astrological considerations are sometimes invoked by individuals in rabbinic stories; and a few discussions focus on whether Israel as a nation is subject to astrological influence.[32] But more direct evidence for Jewish interest in the zodiac in late antiquity comes from the ancient synagogue. In several synagogue mosaic floors, the centerpiece is a zodiac circle, in which Helios, representing the sun, is surrounded by representations of the zodiac signs, depicted as human and animal figures and labeled with the Hebrew equivalents of their names.[33] Likewise, several liturgical poems from Palestine dating to the fifth through eighth centuries CE employ zodiac symbols in their strophic schemes.[34] This evidence, combined with the evidence of the celestial omen texts discussed earlier, indicates that Jews used astrological techniques and written manuals in late antiquity.

Likewise, dream interpretation is essential to biblical narrative. Beginning with the stories of Jacob and Joseph, both biblical and postbiblical literature reflect the premise that dreams are indicators of otherwise unobtainable truths. We lack extensive dream manuals and diaries like those of Aelius Aristides and Artemidorus, not to mention the extensive writing on dream theory by Greek and Roman writers from Aristotle to the church fathers.[35] The rabbis, however, examined dreams and their meaning for ordinary individuals, as discussed later. Moreover, ritual texts for the cultivation of dreams appear in Jewish ritual texts from late antiquity and the early Middle Ages. One genre is that of dream inquiry (*she'elat ḥalom*), rituals intended to cultivate an informing angel who will appear in a dream and answer a given question.[36] These rituals, as well as Talmudic stories (described later) in which the dead appear to a living person, differ from most other types of divination surveyed here in that they rely on an individual, otherworldly figure to reveal secrets to someone on earth. But they also suppose that a person's inner faculties are especially receptive during dreaming, a state the Talmud calls "one-sixtieth of prophecy."[37]

In looking for early evidence for divination, we have seen practices based mostly on celestial events, the human body, and the human soul. We turn now to rabbinic literature, particularly the Talmuds, which offers evidence for other kinds of practices based on everyday events, animals, and objects. We then return to the Genizah and other medieval manuscript sources for books of divination. But when we turn to these sources, we also are turning to another level of interpretation. That is, we must be conscious of what practices are presented and also how they are presented by their authors. We will see that rabbinic literature and divination texts present very different pictures of some of the same ideas.

Forbidden Rites

When we read what rabbinic literature has to say on divination, we must be aware of the legal framework by which that discourse takes place. That is, reports of divinatory activities in the Talmud are often set into legal discussions regarding the interpretation of biblical laws on divination. The evidence from rabbinic literature also includes stories of rabbis, sometimes seeking information through divination for themselves and sometimes interacting with nonrabbinic professionals engaged in divinatory arts. At the same time, the vast scope of rabbinic literature allows for a wide diversity of points of view, including what might be called an "ethnographic" interest in daily life. These stories are discussed here not because they are accurate depictions of historically verifiable events but because they are evidence of practices and social dynamics as their authors saw them.

Because of the legal foundations of this literature, distinguishing between permitted forms of divination and forbidden forms occupies a certain amount of attention. There is much at stake in these definitions, since divination and other forms of direct revelation could constitute a challenge to rabbinic authority. According to a well-known statement in the Babylonian Talmud, "From the day the Temple was destroyed, prophecy has been taken away from the prophets and given to fools and children."[38] This statement, like many others regarding divination in rabbinic literature, would have the effect of discrediting the authority of freestanding prophets and others who might claim to have received messages from divine sources. At the same time, as we will see, the idea that children are the recipients of truths otherwise unavailable to ordinary people was taken seriously in rabbinic civilization.

In particular, legal discussions center on the interpretation of Leviticus 19:26. A terse pronouncement in Sifra, an early Midrashic commentary to Leviticus, gives as examples of forbidden divination those who divine "by mole, by birds, and by stars."[39] Yet as we shall see, bird divination at least was understood to be a legitimate pursuit. Another important legal source is chapters 6 and 7 of the tractate Shabbat in the Tosefta, an early supplement to the Mishnah, and in the Talmuds. This section, known as the chapters on the Ways of the Amorite, seeks to elaborate Leviticus 18:3's commandment against following foreign ritual practices.[40] The result is a list of obscure customs distinguishing which are permitted and which are forbidden according to the Torah. The distinctions between permitted and forbidden practices are so subtle, however, that no modern reader has been able to identify definitively how they are made. Saul Lieberman and Giuseppe Veltri relate this unusual list of practices to known Greco-Roman customs;[41] Yitzhak Avishor suggests that some of the prohibited practices originated in ancient Near Eastern Ritual texts;[42] and Jonathan Seidel argues that the Tosefta's classification serves "to describe 'in-group' practices that needed to be pushed outside the boundaries of society."[43] At any rate, this text also seeks to define the two categories, menaḥesh and me'onen, by representative actions:

> Who is the diviner (menaḥesh)? The one who says: My staff fell from my hand; my bread fell from my mouth; so-and-so called me from behind; a raven called me; a dog bit me; a snake passed to the right of me and a fox to the left of me, and a deer cut me off on my way'" [or], "do not start with me, for it is morning; it is the first of the month; it is Saturday night."[44]

It is possible that the passage is indicating those whose fear of inauspicious occasions prevents them from carrying out everyday activities. At the very least, the statement would discourage the reading of times and events as signaling an individual's fate.

Another classic statement is found in an interesting excursus in the Babylonian Talmud. There Rav is quoted as saying: "Any divination [naḥash] that is not like that of Eliezer the servant of Abraham and Jonathan the son of Saul is not divination."[45]

In Genesis 24:10–14, Abraham's servant, identified in tradition as Eliezer, is sent to find a wife for Isaac. He asks for a specific sign that the chosen woman had arrived, that she give his camels water to drink. In 1 Samuel 14:8–10, Jonathan designated a sign from the Philistine that it was time to attack. As commentators have noted, the statement that these actions are "not divination" is ambiguous.[46] It is not entirely clear whether the divination of Eliezer and Jonathan is to be forbidden. Assuming that it is, the thrust of the statement seems to be that if an action is performed with the specific intention of generating an answer, then it counts as forbidden divination. But if one is simply reading signs from one's environment, the practice is allowable.

The text continues by describing the, presumably acceptable, forms of augury practiced by other sages:

> I. Rav would inquire of ferries; Samuel would inquire into books; Rabbi Yoḥanan would inquire of children.

That is, Rav would wait to see whether a ferry arrived or departed, which would be the omen he sought. Samuel practiced bibliomancy, and Rabbi Yoḥanan practiced a peculiarly rabbinic form of mantic activity: the interpretation of verses recited by children. Remarking that all these practices are different, the text goes on to tell a story of how R. Yoḥanan, having become convinced that Samuel is his superior in learning, decided to visit him:

> II. He said: "I have a master in Babylonia. I will go and see him."
>   A. He said to a child, "Recite your verse."
>   B. He said to him: "Now Samuel had died" (1 Sam. 28:3).
>   C. He said, "This must mean that Samuel has died."

R. Yoḥanan, therefore, had no need to travel to Babylonia. We would seem, then, to have a fine instance of a divinitory practice by which the person solicits a sign, which turns out to have obvious relevance to his life. But here the Talmud adds:

> I. But it was not true. Samuel was not dead; rather it was so that Rabbi Yoḥanan would not bother himself [with the journey].

This small discourse on the subtle distinctions between forbidden and permitted augury turns out not to be a simple lesson in doctrine. First of all, it is difficult to see the distinction between Eliezer's and Jonathan's actions and Yoḥanan's. Furthermore, the Talmud seems to be making a rather sly statement about the results of questioning omens, which, it suggests, may have unintended consequences. In this case, the result is not that Yoḥanan learns the truth but that he is compelled unwittingly, presumably by Heaven, to do what is best for him. It is apparent that like Greek drama, the Talmud's narrative is not above using oracles ironically. That is, the narrative seeks to confound our expectations of the outcome of an oracular inquiry. The message may be that such oracles are not mechanical, independent entities but instruments of the divine will.

This is hardly the only instance of divination by children's recitation in rabbinic literature. For example, often someone will learn something relevant to his or her life while passing a schoolhouse and hearing a verse recited there, as did Rabbi Yoḥanan in b. Hullin 95b.[47] The assumption that children are the special, if unconscious, receptacles of cosmic wisdom is reflected in widespread and ancient divination systems in which a child is made to look into a bowl of liquid or other shiny object. An old Jewish manifestation of this practice is the corpus of oil-divination texts collected by Samuel Daiches.[48] In these texts, a young boy or a pregnant woman smears oil into his or her palm or thumbnail. The result is a vision of a class of informing angels known as the "princes of oil and the princes of the thumb." Sarah Iles Johnston studied the Greco-Roman divination practices in which children play a similar role as informants. In these cases, the idea is that children may have a special receptiveness to oracular apparitions and, at the same time, would be unbiased reporters of their experiences.[49] This notion may also be the idea behind the Talmudic statement quoted earlier that prophecy is given to fools and children. Of course, as Johnston shows, the opposite is the case. Children are particularly susceptible to suggestion and are just as likely to tell the adults what they want to hear.

If we accept the premise underlying the ancient distinction between "technical" and "natural" divination, that the souls of children and the inner faculties of all human beings are sources of supernatural disclosure, then dreams fall under a similar category of divination. Although the Talmud states that "a dream that is not interpreted is like a letter that is not read,"[50] dream interpretation is likewise treated with considerable ambivalence in rabbinic literature. It is the subject of extended essays in the Palestinian and Babylonian Talmuds. The Palestinian Talmud's discussion consists largely of a set of stories in which rabbinic dream interpreters shock their questioners with their interpretations, and as in the story of Yoḥanan and the river omen, the results of dream inquiry turn out in unexpected ways.[51] The Babylonian Talmud contains similar stories and also includes what has been called a "Talmudic dreambook" listing dreams and the means by which they can be interpreted.

These passages have been studied extensively for their complex and sophisticated use of ancient psychology, intricate wordplay, and social ramifications.[52] For example, the rabbinic maxim "All dreams follow their interpretation" has been seen as an ancient antecedent to Freudian interpretation.[53] For our purposes, it is worth noting that as portrayed in these stories, dream interpretation involves a complex interweaving of verbal and symbolic components. As Galit Hasan-Rokem observed, "Dreams are visual experiences that are necessarily transformed into words in order to turn them into meaningful communication."[54]

Rabbinic literature also attests to the practice of fasting so that an angelic figure known as a "man of dreams" (*ish ḥalom*) or "master of dreams" (*ba'al ḥalom*) would come to the practitioner in his sleep.[55] In addition, some stories indicate that the dead indeed know something we do not.[56] In one story, a pious man (*ḥasid*) spends a night in a graveyard and overhears the spirit of a dead person proposing to her neighbor that they "wander out into the world and hear what punishment is coming into the world." Although one of the spirits is unable to travel because she is buried in a reed mat, the other one learns of a coming hailstorm, information by which the pious man can profit.[57] The idea behind this story is the same as that behind Quintus's theory of dreaming: that souls that are not earthbound can converse with one another and thus have access to information hidden from conscious mortals.

Several Talmudic statements and stories pertain to the interpretation of omens (*simanim*) in a person's life, in nature, and in the animal world. A striking case is the set of practices known as the "language of birds and the language of palm trees," in which the patterns of bird flight and song and the swaying of palm trees are read using finely honed techniques. The latter skill was attributed to Yoḥanan ben Zakkai, one of the founders of Rabbinic Judaism, along with the language of angels and demons.[58] Yet even these crafts are not represented without ambivalence in the Talmud. One representation of this tradition in the Babylonian Talmud takes the form of the following story of Rav Ilish, who was in prison:

> One day he was sitting with someone who knew the language of birds. A raven came and called out to him. [Rav Ilish] said to the man, "What did he say?" He said, "Flee, Ilish! Flee Ilish!" He said, "Ravens are liars. I do not rely on them." Then a dove came along and called out. He said [to the man], "What did he say? He said, "Flee, Ilish, Flee Ilish." He said, "The community of Israel is likened to a dove.[59] This must mean that a miracle will happen to me. I will flee."[60]

Mindful perhaps of the biblical Noah story, Rav Ilish does not listen to the raven, which he calls a liar, but to the dove. On the one hand, the raven has the power to predict the future. On the other hand, the raven is known in Talmudic lore as a disgraceful creature who disobeyed Noah's orders on the ark and resented God's treatment of him.[61] Likewise, the Talmud's remark about the informing agents known as the "princes of the egg and the princes of the thumb," like the oil-divination practices collected by Daiches, is instructive: "One may consult the Princes of the Egg and the Princes of the Thumb—but [one does not] because they lie."[62] The assumption behind bird, tree, and angelic divination is that these creatures know something we do not. But by implying that they do not always tell the truth, the Talmud is once again ironically distancing itself from the full ramifications of that assumption. Indeed, the Talmudic objection to the "princes of the thumb" is met head-on in one of Daiches's late medieval texts: "And if they lie, you shall say three times: I adjure you in the name of Sansniel, Pathiel, Shaqiel, that you tell me the truth."[63]

Rabbinic literature is not alone in mistrusting these sources. Zvi Abush cites an Akkadian source that raises the possibility that the gods may not always provide reliable omens.[64] But the way that rabbinic literature uses stories that subvert the divination paradigm is instructive. It is important to understand that the rabbis' ambivalence is not because they were more "rational," "scientific," or "intellectual." Indeed, there is ample evidence that the rabbis were no strangers to divination practices; in fact, they seem to have cultivated a reputation as magical practitioners.[65] Rather, they were far more interested in discrediting competing systems and practitioners of divine authority.

Books of Divination

We return now to the Genizah and other collections of medieval Jewish manuscripts. Several types of divination manuals proliferated in the Middle Ages. Some of these resemble divination books composed in Latin and Greek in late antiquity, but at the same time, these books have much in common with Arabic books for similar purposes.[66] A major category of divinitory technique relies on the body of an individual to relate details about his or her fate. The best-known examples of this category are *physiognomy* and *chiromancy*, the study of facial features and palm reading, respectively. Both are represented in early medieval Jewish literature and can be found in Genizah fragments. The extant fragments of these texts are mostly formulaic and consist of lists of sets of conditions and their interpretations. Besides the Aramaic omen text just described are a few texts of physiognomy and chiromancy studied by Gershom Scholem that are related to the literature of early Jewish mysticism.[67] An ancient genre of divination based on body tremors or twitches, known as *palmomancy*, is known from both Arabic and Judeo-Arabic sources from the Genizah. Esther-Miriam Wagner and Gideon Bohak have made one such text available, a twelfth-century fragment of a Judeo-Arabic twitch-divination manual.[68] They note that in another such fragment, the manual is ascribed to Shem, the son of Noah, as are many Jewish magical and medical texts, and thus is given a Jewish origin.[69]

A fuller literary pattern characterizes another popular example of a genre of divination text: the book of "lots," or *goralot*. Several of them circulate throughout the Jewish world to this day under the titles *Goralot Aḥitofel*, *Sefer Urim ve-Thumim*, and books attributed to the medieval bible commentator Abraham ibn Ezra. These books have become particularly popular in recent years, in part thanks to an entrepreneur and folklorist by the name of Meir Backal, who publishes them in handy miniature editions sold all over Israel and New York, based on readily available manuscripts.[70] These books are usually highly structured, in contrast to the magical handbooks, or *grimoires*, that proliferate in the Genizah and other collections, which are truly miscellanies. They usually consist of the following, several well-delineated parts:

1. A pious, presumably "historical" introduction attesting to the miraculous origins of the book. These introductions are common to magical, technical, and esoteric books and usually associate the techniques in them to a succession of heroes from Israel's history.[71]
2. Instructions for the procedure.
3. A prayer to be recited by the practitioner, which petitions God in pious language to accept his request for information.
4. The raw material, so to speak, of the procedure, laid out in graphic fashion, usually in grids.
5. The technical data—what computer programmers might call an array—listing the various characteristics of the inquirer and his or her fate.

A recent study of the Genizah fragments of these texts shows that they belong to a genre known as *sortes*, a "literary composition which includes a number of sayings independent from one another, each explaining or predicting a fate." These sayings are "written down in such a manner that only one of them may be pointed to if the inquirer follows particular instructions."[72] The books differ in their manner of choosing the particular saying. One common method is the rolling of dice, but the procedure can also consist of placing one's finger randomly on one of a number of lettered squares. These then refer to messages printed in the back of the book. The Genizah versions of these books clearly took shape before the earliest of the existing manuscripts, which date to the tenth century and may have been a bridge between the ancient Greek and Latin oracle texts and medieval traditions.

Other techniques include *geomancy*, which depends on drawing complex diagrams in the sand. A particularly rich sand-divination text going directly back to an Islamic model is currently being studied by Yael Okun of the Jewish National Library.[73] There also are weather omens, divination by body tremors, and even a text discovered by Martin S. Cohen describing what is called "*hashlakhat esba'ot*, or the 'throwing of fingers,'" evidently an antecedent of a well-known children's game.[74] The Mishnah states that priests who were to clear the altar of ashes in the ancient Temple were chosen by a procedure in which each priest extended either one or two fingers and an official counted them off, arriving at a designated number. The idea is that because no one could predict how many fingers each priest would extend, the procedure contained an element of randomness.[75] These texts, then, offer systems of interpretations in which seemingly random acts, the weather, involuntary body movements and the like are given cosmic significance.

If the authors of these books of Jewish divination were aware of rabbinic reservations about augury, they do not betray it. By and large, these books hark back to older forms of authority. This is done in their introductions, particularly through the use of *historiolae*, brief stories or historical references used to validate the magic. Often they claim that the praxis described in the book can act as a substitute for a lost ritual in the Temple. These books usually include a prayer to be recited by the practitioner before inquiring about the divination system. In one Genizah fragment, TS K1.131, which is similar to a common book known as *Goralot Ahitofel* (*The Oracles of Ahitophel*), the introductory prayer emphasizes that the petitioner will not use them in order to "transgress the Torah and what is written in it" and expresses the hope that the community will be among those who hold fast to the Torah. The petitioner asks to use the oracle because

we have neither prophet nor priest to inquire of the Urim and Thumim. Therefore, I approach you and rely on your abundant mercy in inquiring of these oracles for every matter, to inform humanity of your ways; they[76] will thank you for all your works, whether good or bad, whether healing or sickness, whether deprivation or abundance, as it is written: "I shall raise the cup of salvation and call on the name of the Lord; I shall find trouble and agony, and call out the name of the Lord."[77]

Here the author states explicitly that the text's divination system can substitute for the Urim and Thumim in the Temple. This line of rhetoric conforms to a pattern common to magical rituals, that in the absence of a specific Temple ritual, the esoteric technique is available to all who possess it.[78]

Chance, Destiny, and Signification

What do the sources described here contribute to the idea of a nontextual semiotics of ancient Judaism? For the Dadaists, random operations were significant precisely for the disorder they produced. John Cage, it seems, would have us think of the results produced by random operations as a higher order of the reality already inherent in the environment. By contrast, our diviners wished to tune in to messages encoded in the sequence of things. To do this, they created highly formalized technologies that they claimed were available to only a few and yet accessible to all who would patronize them. These ritualized disciplines translated the signs all around them into texts that would be relevant to their clients. At the same time, the disciplines that they created, like the chance operations of the modern artists and composers, sought to subsume the individual will to a larger force, in this case, the divine will. Thus asking a child to recite the verse he had been studying allows for a verbal reply to a question, but not one that is consciously keyed in to the meaning of the question. Using motion, gravity, or natural events to determine signification likewise selects the medium but not the message. The purpose of these procedures, which distance the practitioner from his or her will, is ostensibly to ensure a kind of objectivity—that the resulting answer is not a product of the inquirer's wishful thinking but a genuine reflection of the "chance" occurrence.

In these procedures we also find a fluid relationship between verbal and nonverbal communication. Although such divination manuals as the Book of the Urim and Thumim and the Book of Ahitophel used the Torah to validate themselves, they also remind the reader and participant of a cultic form of divine disclosure, in which the locus of revelation is not the text but the object, and the priest, not the sage, is the curator of the hermeneutical tradition. So, too, astrological and natural omen practices participate in a long scholastic tradition that relies on texts for their continuity and methods. At the same time, the ultimate sources of these revelations lie beyond the text.

Divination techniques reflect a particular worldview in a deeper way. Divination is a system in which every detail of our environment is filled with meaning. That is, to the diviner the world is inherently semiotic. As the next chapter shows, this conception has wider implications for how ancient Jews saw discrete elements of that environment and their relationship to the divine.

Bubbling Blood and Rolling Bones

The first-century Jewish historian Josephus, quoting a book attributed to a writer named Hecataeus, tells a story of a Jewish archer named
Mosollamus, who was traveling with the Ptolemaic army. At one point the
army stopped marching because a bird was flying overhead and the military
soothsayer wanted to observe it:

> The seer having pointed out the bird to him, and saying that if it [the bird]
> stays there, it is expedient for all to wait still longer, and if it rises and flies
> ahead, to advance, but if [it flies] behind, to withdraw at once, he [Mosol-
> lamus], after keeping silence and drawing his bow, shot and, hitting the
> bird, killed [it]. When the seer and some others became irritated and
> called down curses upon him, he [Mosollamus] said: "Why are you raving,
> [you] wretches?" Then, taking the bird in his hands he said: "How, then,
> could this [bird], which did not provide for its own safety, say anything
> sound about our march? For had it been able to know the future, it would
> not have come to this place, fearing that Mosollamus the Jew would draw
> his bow and kill it."[1]

This story is a criticism of one assumption that underlies the practice of divination, the idea that animals and objects possess knowledge and will that
allow them to signify to human beings. We have seen that divination traditions presuppose a world alive with meaning, in which any creature or object
can serve as a signifier. In ancient Judaism, this idea is reinforced by several
legends that ascribe agency to elements of the natural world. This chapter
explores this conception.

In rabbinic literature, folklore, and piyyut, several sources ascribe agency
and intentionality to natural components of creation. In some cases, these
are revealed to be the result of a divine plan according to which God embedded objects, living creatures, and natural substances in the world so that they
could fulfill a purpose in later history. In other cases, they are understood as

inherent in the nature of such substances as blood and earth. We have seen that Midrash and related sources state that several components of present-day reality were created before the world itself, or perhaps had been coexistent with God or an element of his being, and that in particular, the Tabernacle, the Temple, and their cult were precreated and serve as a model for future history. This idea is significant because it locates a ritual institution in the primordial history of the world. As we saw in chapter 3, similar lists of things created in the twilight between end of the six days of creation and the first Sabbath were drawn up as well. The following is the full text of that list from Mishnah Avot 5:6:

I. Ten things were created on the eve of the Sabbath at twilight:
  A. The mouth of the earth (that swallowed up Korah);[2]
  B. the mouth of the well (from which the Israelites drank in the wilderness);[3]
  C. the mouth of (Balaam's) ass;
  D. the rainbow;
  E. manna;
  F. (Moses's) rod;
  G. the *Shamir*;[4]
  H. The letters (of the Hebrew alphabet);
  I. the writing (on the tablets of the Ten Commandments);
  J. and the tablets (of the Ten Commandments).
  K. And some say:
    1. also demons;
    2. the grave of Moses;
    3. and the ram of Abraham our father.[5]
  L. And some say: Also the tongs, (which can only be) made by tongs.[6]

Most of these items are miraculous objects or creatures that were to serve in the history of Israel later on. The only items that do not feature in specific historical episodes of the nation's history are Hebrew letters, demons, and the first tongs. Hebrew letters are unique as elements of creation, having vied with one another according to another legend for priority in creation and, at the same time, are the building blocks of textuality.[7] Demons are pervasive forces that act on nature; and tongs are essential to civilization.[8] This motif thus reflects a teleological view of creation in which God embeds materials, beings, and objects in the world with specific historical intentions. In ancient and medieval Jewish exegesis, poetry, and folklore, this teleology is expressed in two ways. The idea that precreated things are to be used or interpreted at a later time and that ostensibly inarticulate beings or substances may act out the divine will or exercise moral judgment.

This chapter examines two ramifications of this teleological frame of mind, the idea that substances like blood and the earth serve as actors in the moral drama of history, as well as the role that animals and inanimate objects play in enacting or resisting the divine will. This chapter thus explores one of the implications of the idea of divination in Judaism, the idea that God has embedded meaning and agency in animals, objects, and the elements of the natural world.

The Voice of Blood

Blood is ostensibly an inanimate substance. But in ancient Mediterranean cultures, the nature of blood and its fate had ritual, legal, and cosmic consequences. In his classic study of impurity in Greek religion, Robert Parker shows how the shedding of blood was both a social and a metaphysical concern.[9] In ancient Greek society, the unjust spilling of blood creates an imbalance that must be addressed through legal redress and sacrifice. On the one hand, as Parker states, "Murder-pollution is caused by an unnatural act, and for this reason is virtually identified . . . with the anger of the man unnaturally killed."[10] On the other hand, it is a "vehicle through which social disruption is expressed."[11]

In Jewish thought, blood is identified with life itself; a law in Leviticus 17:11 forbids the eating of blood. The reason given is that "the life of the flesh is in the blood, and I have assigned it to you for making expiation for your lives upon the altar; it is the blood, as life, that effects expiation"; similarly, Genesis 9:4 forbids all humanity to eat of "flesh with its life-blood in it," and Israelite dietary laws require the draining of blood from animals during slaughtering.[12] So, too, the consequences of shedding blood are both social and metaphysical in ancient Judaism. Thus when God challenges Cain regarding his murder of Abel, he declares, "Your brother's blood cries out to Me from the ground. Therefore you shall be more cursed than the ground, which opened its mouth to receive your brother's blood from your hand" (Gen. 4:10–11). Genesis 4:10 uses the plural, *dame*, for blood. This presumed anomaly was the basis for the homily that, according to the Mishnah, was used by judges as an admonition to impress on witnesses the gravity of giving honest testimony in capital cases:

I. Know that capital cases are not like monetary cases:
   A. In monetary cases, a person pays money and makes atonement.
   B. But in capital cases, the blood (of the accused) and the blood of his descendents depend on (the witness) to the end of the world.
II. For thus we have found in the case of Cain when he killed his brother, as it is written, "the bloods of your brother (*dame aḥikhah*) cry out."
   A. It does not say, "the blood (*dam*) of your brother, but "the bloods of your brother"—his blood and the blood of his descendants.
   B. Another interpretation: "The bloods of your brother"—for his blood was spilled on the trees and on the rocks. (M. Sanh. 4:5)

This speech distinguishes at I the consequences of capital cases and those cases in which monetary payment constitutes restitution. In order to make this point, it engages in two exegeses of Genesis 4:11 in II. The first (II A) takes the plural to mean that the accusation of murder (and, by extension, false witness) applies to the blood of the victim and also the victim's descendants, who will never be born. The second interpretation (II B) implies that the earth refused to accept Abel's blood and that therefore it was scattered above the earth. A comment in Genesis Rabbah explains: "'Your brother's blood cries out to Me from the ground' (Gen. 4:10): It could not ascend because his soul had not yet ascended, and it could not go down, because no person had ever been buried there (in the earth), so his blood was spilled on the trees and rocks."[13] These latter interpretations thus contradict what would seem to be the plain meaning of scripture, which states that the earth swallowed up the blood and was cursed.[14] In the anonymous Avodah piyyut "Az be-En Kol," the earth is cursed according to the conventional meaning of the verse:[15]

> You shall surely be
> a destructive curse
> along with that which opened its mouth[16]
> to share that which you stole.[17]

The implication is that not only did Cain steal Abel's blood but so did the earth, since it accepted it.

In the Mekhilta de-Rabbi Ishmael, an early rabbinic commentary to Exodus, two interpretations of Exodus 15:12 consider the implications of the earth's acceptance of the blood of Cain:

I. "[You put out Your right hand,] the earth swallowed them" (Exod. 15:12):

    A. By what merit were they given a grave? Because they said, "The Lord is in the right" (Exod. 9:27).

    B. The Holy One, blessed be He, said, You have accepted judgment upon yourselves, so I will not deprive you of your reward and I will give you a place to be buried, as it is said, "You put out Your right hand, the earth swallowed them."

II. Another interpretation: "You put out Your right hand, the earth swallowed them."

    A. This teaches that the sea tossed them to the dry land and the dry land tossed them into the sea.

    B. The dry land said:

        1. "Since I accepted only the blood of Abel, who was an individual, and it was said to me, 'Cursed is the earth' (Gen. 4:11), now how can I accept the blood of these troops until God swears to me that He will not take me to court?"

        2. As it is written, "You put out Your right hand, the earth swallowed them," and "right hand" means an oath, as it is written, "The Lord has sworn by His right hand" (Isa. 62:8).[18]

Both interpretations are predicated on the idea that the earth should refuse to accept a guilty person. In the first interpretation, the Egyptian soldiers are given a burial place, according to Exodus 15:12, because Pharaoh had admitted God's justice in Exodus 12:27. In the second interpretation, the sea worries that since the earth was cursed because it accepted Abel's blood, it will likewise be brought to justice if it accepts the Egyptians. In the Babylonian Talmud (b. Pes. 118b),[19] a different explanation is offered for why the sea tossed the Israelites onto dry land:

I. "They rebelled at the sea" (Ps. 106:7):

    A. This teaches that Israel rebelled at that time and said, "Just as we are rising from one side (of the sea), so are the Egyptians rising from the other side."

    B. The Holy One, blessed be He said to the Prince of the Sea, "Spit them out to dry land."

        1. He said before Him, "Master of the World! Is there a servant whose master gives a gift to him and takes it back?"

2. He said to him, "I will give you one and a half times as many of them."
3. He said before Him, "Master of the World! Is there a servant who claims a debt from his master?"
4. He said to him, "Let the river of Kishon be my guarantee."

C. Immediately he spit them out to the dry land, and Israel came and saw them, as it is said, "Israel saw the Egyptians dead on the shore of the sea" (Exod. 14:30).

The Israelites could not believe that the Egyptians had perished in the sea, so God commanded the Prince of the Sea (the angel appointed over the sea) to spit them out to dry land so they could see that they were dead. In B, the Prince of the Sea complains that God has taken back the "gift" of the Egyptian dead that he has given him. God replies that he will repay the Prince with Sisera's troops, who were swept away into the Kishon and out to sea, according to Judges 5:20. This interpretation ascribes agency not to the sea itself but to an angelic figure or "prince" in charge of its administration. Moreover, unlike the previous stories, it also implies that the sea is both willing and eager to accept the dead bodies of the Egyptians.

A story that appears in the Palestinian Talmud, Palestinian midrashic sources, and the Babylonian Talmud illustrates a dramatic consequence of the beliefs in the agency of blood and the earth.[20] According to 2 Chronicles 24:20–22, a prophet named Zechariah, son of Jehoiada, was murdered in the Temple Court at the command of King Joash for prophesying against the kingdom of Judah. As he was dying, Zechariah called for God to avenge his murder.[21] The Talmudic story seems to connect this episode to the destruction of the first Temple 250 years later by the army of Nebuchadnezzar, king of Babylon, and his officer, Nebuzaradan (2 Kings 25:8–21). The earliest versions occur in the Palestinian Talmud and Midrash Pesiqta de-Rav Kahana. There are many significantly different details in the Babylonian Talmud's version. In turn, that version influenced the versions in later Palestinian Midrashim. In addition, there are striking parallels to this story in Christian sources, especially in Ethiopian Christian exegetical literature.[22] The version in the Palestinian Talmud and Pesiqta de-Rav Kahana is in Hebrew, with the exception of one unit, Nebuzaradan's chastisement to the blood of Zechariah (unit E), which is in Aramaic. In contrast, most of the Babylonian Talmud's version is in Aramaic, with two passages, including Nebuzaradan's charge to the blood, in Hebrew.[23]

The Palestinian Talmud's version is quoted here, and a few significant details added by the Babylonian Talmud and the Palestinian midrashim are noted. In most sources, the story is introduced by a statement that eighty thousand young priests were killed because of the blood of Zechariah. The question is then raised exactly where in the Temple Zechariah was killed:

I.   R. Yudan asked R. Aḥa, "Where was Zechariah killed, in the Women's Court or the Court of the Israelites?"
   A. He said to him, "Not in the Court of the Israelites, nor in the Women's Court, but in the Court of the Priests."

This leads to a discussion of exactly what was done with the blood:

   B. Nor did they did not treat his blood like the blood of a deer, nor like the blood of a ram.
      1. In that case (that of a wild animal) it is written, "[If any Israelite or any stranger who resides them hunts down and animal or a bird that may be eaten,] he shall pour out its blood and cover it with earth" (Lev. 17:13).
      2. But in this case (the killing of the prophet), it is written, "[For the blood she shed is still in her]; she set it upon a bare rock; [she did not pour it out on the ground to cover it with earth]" (Ezek. 24:7).
      3. Why all this? "She set her blood upon the bare rock so that it was not covered, so that it may stir up [My] fury to take vengeance" (Ezek. 24:8).

To highlight the enormity of the crime, the Talmud adds:

   C. Seven sins were committed that day: They killed a priest, a prophet, and a judge;[24] they spilled innocent blood; they polluted the Temple Court; and it occurred on Sabbath and the Day of Atonement.[25]

At this point the story of the murder of the priests follows.

II. When Nebuzaradan[26] went up (to the Temple Mount), he saw the blood boiling.
   A. He said to them, "What kind (of blood) is this?" They said to him, "The blood of the bulls, rams, and lambs that we used to slaughter on the altar."
   B. Immediately they brought to him bulls, rams, and lambs and slaughtered them for him. But the blood was still boiling.

Bubbling Blood and Rolling Bones | 81

C. And since they did not admit to him, he hung them on the gallows (to be tortured).
  1. They said, "(It is) because the Holy One, blessed be He, wants to claim his blood from our hands."
  2. They said to him, "It is the blood of the priest, prophet, and judge, who prophesied to concerning [all that you would do to us],[27] and we stood over him and killed him.
D. Immediately he brought eighty thousand young priests and killed them over it. But still the blood boiled.[28]
E. Then he (Nebuzaradan) chastised it. He said to it, "What do you want me to do—destroy your entire people because of you?"
F. Immediately the Holy One, blessed be He, was filled with mercy and said, "If this man, who is flesh and blood and cruel, is filled with mercy for my children, how much more so should I be, about whom it is written, 'For the Lord your God is a compassionate God; He will not fail you nor will He let you perish; He will not forget the covenant which Heb made on oath with your fathers?'" (Deut. 4:31).
G. Immediately He signaled to the blood and it was swallowed up in its place.

This complex story of martyrdom and revenge has many dimensions. The following analysis focuses on the function of blood and earth. One of the questions this story raises is whether the blood of the martyr can be compared with sacrificial blood, a question implied in the discussion in I of where the prophet was killed. In 2 Chronicles 24:21 we read that he was killed "in the Court of the House of the Lord," suggesting that he was killed in one of the outer courts in the temple complex. R. Aḥa's answer in I A, that he was killed in the Court of the Priests, emphasizes that Zechariah was killed in the section of the Temple where the sacrificial slaughter takes place.[29] This raises the question implied in I B, whether his blood was disposed of in a way analogous to that of game animals—that is, following, in a perverse way, some kind of sacral law. The answer given in I B 1–3, that his blood was spilled on the rocks, serves to draw a sharp distinction between the blood of a sacrificial or alimentary animal and the blood of the martyr. The citation of Ezekiel 24 in I B 2–3 highlights the prospect that the blood of the prophet will arouse God's revenge.[30]

Likewise, in II A–B, the Jerusalemites' attempt to deceive Nebuzaradan into thinking that the blood is that of sacrificial animals has the effect of distinguishing the blood of sacrifices from the blood of martyrs. One version in the Babylonian Talmud, which adds to the drama of the earlier story in several ways, reinforces this distinction.[31] In this version, Nebuzaradan does not simply slaughter the sacrificial animals to appease the blood; rather, he kills them to find out whether sacrificial blood will boil under normal circumstances. When he does so, he sees that their blood does not boil, indicating to him that sacrificial blood does not usually act in this way. In II C of our source, once it becomes clear that this is no ordinary blood, Nebuzaradan then demands, on threat of torture, to know why this blood is boiling (II C).[32] When he is told that it is the blood of the prophet, he begins to appease it by slaughtering young priests in II D, which, however, does not appease the blood.[33] Eventually he speaks directly to the blood (or Zechariah himself) in E.[34] Only when he threatens to wipe out the entire nation does God have mercy and stop the blood from boiling (F–G).

As folklorists George Kohut and Tamar Alexander-Frizer point out, the premise of this story and others like it is that blood has a conscious, living identity with the person from whom it flows.[35] But this is also related to an idea implied by Genesis 4:11 and interpretations of it, that the earth itself may refuse to accept the blood of a victim of murder. In this story, therefore, there are three types of agency beyond that of living humans: (1) the agency of blood, which takes it upon itself to act on behalf of the dead person from which it came to extract justice; (2) the agency of the earth, which refuses to accept the blood of the innocent; and (3) the agency of the will of God, who intervenes when provoked by the boundless evil of the Babylonian villain to stop the natural process of revenge.[36] In the Babylonian Talmud's version, the story has a happy ending. Nebuzaradan, horrified at the bloodshed that he has caused, reasons, "If this can happen to them (the Jews), who only killed one man, what will happen to me?" He then flees the scene and converts to Judaism.[37]

Richard Kalmin has conducted a detailed analysis of this story and argues that the versions in Rabbinic literature were adapted from a non-rabbinic Hebrew source, probably originating in Jewish Christian circles.[38] He argues furthermore that the earliest version of the story emphasized God's abandonment of the Jews but that by adding the general's rebuke of Zechariah and his blood in Aramaic (II E in this outline), the rabbis transformed it into a tale of God's ultimate mercy toward Israel. For our purposes, Kalmin's arguments raise the prospect that this story originated outside rabbinic circles and emphasize that the story was at least was told in some form outside those circles. If so, we can see this conception of the peculiar characteristics of the blood of the righteous not simply as reflective of the ideology of a few storytellers but also emblematic of a more pervasive worldview.

Useful Animals

A second category of tales about the active role of seemingly mute entities concerns animals and objects that act out the divine will in crucial moments in history. Greek and Roman mythologies are replete with myths about animals, especially those in which interactions and metamorphoses between animals and humans are common.[39] These kinds of myths are rarer in ancient Jewish myths, but animals do sometimes play a role. Victor Aptowitzer cataloged stories in which animals are punished for their misdeeds or, conversely, repent of their misdeeds by helping a biblical hero or harming a villain.[40] In other stories, the moon and stars or mountains vie for primacy or for God's favor. One common myth is that God shrank the moon because of its arrogance;[41] another is that the mountains of the world vied among themselves for the honor of being the site where the Ten Commandments were given.[42] In another category, animals and impersonal substances act as the agents of divine retribution.[43]

One such story appears in Leviticus Rabbah, the Midrash to Lamentations and parallels.[44] Like the story of the blood of Zechariah, it is also an elaborate, violent story of destiny and revenge. In it, Titus, destroyer of Jerusalem, enters the Temple and desecrates it in the most unspeakably obscene ways. In revenge, God destroys him in a gruesome way through the tiniest of His creatures, a mosquito. Galit Hasan-Rokem analyzed this story from the perspective of folklore studies.[45] Her analysis sheds light on how its structure suggests, as she puts it, a "mediation of the contradiction inherent in a situation in which an omnipotent deity's abode lies in the ashes of a fire lit by an emperor subsequently killed by a mosquito."[46] Hasan-Rokem uses the story to stress the theme of the limits of God's omnipotence. This story also is useful to our discussion of the theme of the teleological selection of objects and animals in creation. Placing this story in its redactional context illustrates this point.

In Leviticus Rabbah, this story is introduced by a discussion of whether God has created anything unnecessary.[47] The exegetical starting point for this discussion is Eccles. 5:8, which is taken by the midrash to mean "And the superfluity (ve-yitron) of all the earth is His; He controls a field that is cultivated."[48] The subsequent exegeses of this verse stress the necessity of every detail of creation. According to one statement, "Even things in the world that seem to you superfluous, such as fiber to make ropes, fibers to weave a cord[49]—even they are for the benefit of the world."[50] Another interpretation explains that even bothersome insects are necessary: "'And the superfluity of the earth is His' (Eccles 5:8): Even things that you see as superfluous to the world, such as flies, mosquitoes, and fleas—even they are (included) in the creation of the world, as it is written, 'And the heaven and earth were completed'" (Gen. 2:1).[51] The midrash then proceeds to expound on the moral implications of the remainder of the verse from Ecclesiastes. The unit that follows restates and interprets the verse from Ecclesiastes, which serves to introduce the story of Titus and the mosquito:

I. "And the advantage of the earth is His" (Eccles 5:8):
   A. The Holy One, blessed be He, said to the prophets, "If you will not convey my message, I have no messengers."
   B. R. Aḥa said: The Holy One, blessed be He, carries out his message with anything—even by means of a snake, even by means of a scorpion, even by means of a frog, even by means of a mosquito.[52]

The word translated as "message" can also refer to a commission or errand. That is, God uses whatever creatures are necessary to do his bidding. The saga of Titus and the mosquito then follows:

II. The evil Titus entered the Holy of Holies, his sword sheathed in his hand, and cut the two curtains.
   A. Then he took two prostitutes, spread out a Torah scroll under them, and had sexual intercourse with them on top of the altar;
   B. his sword came out dipped in blood.
      1. Some say it was the blood of the Holy of Holies, and some say it was the blood of the goat of Yom Kippur.

As the story begins, Titus destroys the Temple, the physical habitation of God on earth, and then desecrates it in the most obscene and violent way. First he slashes the curtain that covers the Holy of Holies; the story may imply that Titus thought the blood on the sword was the blood of the Deity himself.[53] He then taunts God further:

   C. He then cursed on high and said, "One who does battle with a king in the desert and is victorious is not like one who does battle with a king in his own palace and is victorious over him."[54]
   D. What did he do? He gathered all the vessels of the Temple, placed them in a net, and sent down to a ship.
   E. When he went down, he ran into a gale on the sea.

1. He said, "It seems to me that the god of this people is only powerful in water. He did not punish the generation of the flood
   except with water; he did not punish the generation of the Tower
   of Babel except with water; he did not destroy the Pharaoh and
   all his army except with water.
2. So too, when I was in his house and in his territory, he could not
   prevail against me. But now he has preceded me here."

As in the story of Jonah, divine displeasure is expressed by the stormy
sea. But Titus uses even this struggle against him to belittle the power of his
adversary. Using examples from biblical history, he reasons in E 1 that God
has power only over water. As Galit Hasan-Rokem suggests, Titus under-
stands God as a counterpart to Neptune, who rules over the sea.[55] This is the
point at which God prepares his revenge:

F. The Holy One, blessed be He, said to him, "By your life! I will use
   the smallest creature of all those that I have created from the six
   days of creation to punish that evil man."
G. Immediately the Holy One, blessed be He, signaled[56] to the sea, and
   it stopped raging.
H. When he got to Rome, the people of Rome came out to praise him
   as "Conqueror of the Barbarians!"[57]
   1. Immediately they heated up the bath and he went in to bathe.
   2. When he emerged, they poured him an after-bath double cup[58]
      (of wine).
I. Then God appointed a mosquito, which entered his nostril and kept
   on eating until it reached his brain, and it gnawed at his brain.
   1. He said, "Call the doctors and let them split open the brain of
      this evil man[59] so that I can know by what means the god of this
      people is punishing this evil man."
   2. Immediately they called the doctors, and they split open his
      brain and found a creature in it the size of a young dove and its
      weight was two litras.
      a. R. Lazar b. R. Yose said, "I was there and they put the dove on
         one side of a scale and two litras on the other, and one bal-
         anced out the other."[60]
J. Then they took it and put it into a bowl, and every way [in which]
   one (the mosquito) changed, the other (Titus) changed.
K. The mosquito flew away, [and] the soul of the evil Titus flew away.

This complex story conveys many themes concerning divine power, familiarity and foreignness, and the nature of the soul. The echoes of the Jonah story in D–H are evident both in this tragicomic reversal of Jonah's experience with the ship and its virtuous pagan sailors, as Hasan-Rokem observes,[61] and in God's appointing of the tiny mosquito in I–J—itself a parodic inversion of the big fish that protected Jonah. The story then acquires a somewhat different emphasis once it is seen in its redactional context.

In Leviticus Rabbah, this story is followed by several less dramatic stories regarding the miraculous properties and deeds of animals and objects that have been designated to accomplish a given task on earth.[62] The outcomes of these actions are less consequential than those in the Titus story, but these stories are similarly organized around the rubric that God accomplishes his goals through the most unlikely creatures. They concern a man, usually a rabbi, who observes an unusual phenomenon and concludes that the creature or object he is watching is "prepared to do His (God's) bidding." As Eli Yassif observes, these stories convey a distinctive message on their own and affect the meaning of the Titus legend in its context: "The emphasis thus shifts from punishment of the blasphemer to the story of the smallest of animals carrying out the will of God."[63] Each of these stories uses an unusual or counterintuitive detail about nature to make its point. A particularly striking example is a story about a frog and a scorpion:

> There is a story of a man who was standing on the riverbank and saw a frog carrying a scorpion across the river. He said, "This one is prepared to do (God's) bidding." He (the frog) brought it over the river and went and did His bidding and came and returned it (the scorpion) to its place.[64]

In another version of this story in the later Midrash Tanḥuma, a local detail is added and the purpose of the scorpion's journey is made explicit:

> There is a story of a scorpion that went to do His bidding across the Jordan, and the Holy One, blessed be He, appointed a frog and it carried it over. Then that scorpion stung a man and he died.[65]

Here the scorpion has obviously crossed the river for the explicit purpose of killing someone. In addition, the Tanḥuma's version uses the verb *zimmen*, "appointed," as in the Titus story, to indicate God's designation of a creature for a specific purpose.

Both versions of this story may be related to a common tale of the frog or turtle and the scorpion. This type of folktale, designated in Stith Thompson's *Motif-Index of Folk-Literature* as "Ungrateful river passenger kills carrier from within," appears in Indian, Persian, Syriac, and Arabic sources.[66] In most versions of this story, the scorpion makes a deal with the frog or turtle that he should carry him across the river and assures him that it is not in the scorpion's interest to sting the frog, since they both would drown. The scorpion stings the frog anyway, because, after all, it is a scorpion. The point of the conventional fable is that some creatures (or people) cannot change what they are. In this variation of the story, it is precisely the fact that the scorpion goes against its natural instincts that makes the event remarkable and clearly a sign of divine planning.

In another story in this cycle in Leviticus Rabbah, it is a snake that carries out the mission:

> R. Yanai was sitting and teaching at the gate of the city and saw a snake approaching excitedly.[67] He chased after it from one side and it would one return from the other side. He said, "This one is ready to do His bidding." At once a report spread in the city that so-and-so the son of so-and-so was bitten by a snake and died.[68]

These stories do not constitute the elaborate morality tale of genocide and justice that are the Zechariah and Titus stories but are tales about the fate of ordinary people. Other stories in this series concern the fate of a community or a prominent Jewish leader. The previous story is one of several in this cycle concerning snakes. Another story in this cycle in Leviticus Rabbah also concerns a snake and a rabbi:

> Lazar was sitting and "going about his business"[69] on the toilet and a Roman made him get up and took his place. He said, "This is not in vain." At once a snake came out and struck and killed the Roman. He applied the verse, "I gave men in exchange for you" (Isa 43:4) as "I gave Edom in exchange for you."[70]

Here Lazar's conclusion that his humiliation by the Roman officer is for the best is vindicated by what happens to him. He interprets Isaiah 43:4 to fit his case, revocalizing *adam*, "men," as *Edom*, a codeword in rabbinic literature for Rome. The midrash then rereads the verse to apply to Lazar, for whom God substituted a Roman soldier to be killed by a snake. The next story concerns an entire Jewish community:

R. Yitzhak was sitting at the sea wall of Caesarea and saw a thigh bone rolling. He placed it aside and it kept on rolling. He said, "This (bone) is prepared to do His bidding." After a few days a courier passed by. It rolled between his legs, he tripped on it and fell and died. They went and searched him and found that he was carrying evil decrees against the Jews of Caesarea.[71]

This story concerns not the agency of an animal but of a thigh bone— although it may be that like blood, the thigh bone retains some of the will of the living creature from which it came. Nonetheless, like Titus's mosquito, it does take action in defense of a community. In all cases, the stories make the point that God sends messengers to do his bidding but that if something is destined to happen, nature itself will be determined to make it happen. The word "prepared," *mukhan*, used in these stories, implies both preparation and readiness—that it is ready to do God's will and that it has been explicitly made by God for that purpose. In other words, it implies both divine intent in creation and the agency of the being that carries out that intent.

Creation and Divination

Another way in which animals and objects play an active role is in divination. Divination is a system that presupposes that animals, plants, and inanimate objects are active instruments of communication between God and humanity. This idea is reinforced by the legends described earlier that ascribe agency to elements of the natural world.

In some narrative traditions, divination implies both that the divine employs animals and objects as messengers to humankind and that those beings are active agents. A dramatic example is the story, discussed in the previous chapter, of Rav Ilish, who was in prison and refused to listen to the raven, because "ravens are liars."[72] The assumption behind bird, tree, and angelic divination is that these creatures know something we do not. But in this story asserting that the raven does not always tell the truth, the Talmud also presupposes that it knew what it was saying. As the anecdote about Mosollamus that begins this chapter attests, the idea that animals and other natural phenomena lead conscious existences that reflect their will and destiny did not go unchallenged in antiquity. The story of the skeptical archer circulated in various forms in the Roman world.[73] Both divination techniques and their critics shared the cultural space of the ancient Mediterranean. Jewish culture of that time and place partook of that culture, so we should neither attribute the proliferation of these concepts to foreign influence nor consider them exclusively Jewish. Rather, they are examples of a pervasive way of thinking about the presence of signifiers in the everyday world and the mechanics of that signification.

Agency and Teleology

The wide variety of legends, sayings, and interpretations presented in this chapter indicate a complex relationship among myth, ideology, and mentality. On the one hand, they presuppose a divine creator whose plan for humanity, and for Israel in particular, is inherent in the act of embedding objects, creatures, and natural elements in creation. On the other hand, these sources do not presuppose absolute predestination. The snakes, mosquitoes, bones, and blood that populate these stories act not only out of obedience to divine command but also from an active sense of *telos*.[74] They thus possess agency, if not exactly human will and cunning. These conceptions constitute something deeper than an explicit theology; they constitute a *mentalité* as well. This is evident from the smaller stories of how creatures act out—and act against—their nature to complete the fate of an individual rather than for the benefit of an entire nation. These legends reflect the worldview underlying divination and other forms of nontextual reading, in which God is responsible not only for creating the physical world but also for communicating to humanity through that world.

Conclusions

The Signifying Creator

We have seen that ancient Jews looked not only to the Torah for meaning but to the created world as well. As a consequence they saw a complex world of images, animate and inanimate beings, and events as potential signifiers. We must consider this conception in light of the tendency to see classical Judaic thought as inherently pantextual. The alternative creation myths provided a metaphysical and theological rationale for seeing the physical world as intentionally meaningful; the priestly vestments were understood to constitute a complex system of communication between Israel and the divine realm; and the technical level of divination manuals attests as well to a well-developed and systematic hermeneutic of the natural world, which reflects a worldview expressed in legends regarding the agency of natural elements, animals, and plants and their willingness to act out the historical roles set out for them by God.

At the same time, each of these phenomena manifests a complex relationship between textuality and nontextuality. The midrashim that attest to the idea of the precreation of the Tabernacle and Temple and its ritual system stand in parallel to the myth of the precreated Torah. In fact, a few of those sources take as their exegetical basis the same association with Proverbs 8. The myth that these sources reflect, however, is based on the ancient idea of the Temple as a microcosm of the celestial abode of the god, a paradigm of the function of humankind in serving the gods. This idea is at least as old as the idea of primordial wisdom that informs the pantextual myth of the Torah as the blueprint for the world. Likewise, the complex systems of signification associated with the vestments of the high priest in midrash and synagogue poetry are based on the garments as described in Exodus 28 and 39. Behind these extensive discourses on the beauty, function, and meaning of the vestments stands a memory of the high priest in his dazzling garments as one of the most visually striking features of the Temple. This memory is preserved in Greco-Jewish sources such as Philo and Josephus and the book of Ben Sira and the Avodah piyyutim influenced by it. Jewish divination traditions range from those based explicitly on visual sources, objects, or events, such as the flight patterns of birds, visions obtained by looking into liquids, and the arrival of ferries; to orally based manifestations of textuality, such as the recitation of verses by schoolchildren, to bibliomancy. The relationships between textual and divinatory hermeneutics also serve to show the pedigree of nontextual systems of meaning in antiquity. Finally, legends like the story of the boiling blood of the prophet Zechariah are nominally based on biblical episodes but go well beyond them in their conception of the agency of substances, animals, and objects and their willingness to carry out the divine plan. These phenomena are therefore not limited by the boundaries of textuality and can be seen to stand outside the text.

The association of divinitory and textual systems of meaning is not new. As Jonathan Z. Smith argues, both textual canons and divinitory lists require hermeneutical traditions, personnel, and sensitivity to a community's needs.[1] No less cogent is Zvi Abusch's remarkable demonstration of the consonance between the Akkadian term *Alaktu*, meaning "oracular decision," and the rabbinic term *halakhah*, "legal procedure or decision."[2] For Akkadian literature, as he puts it,

> the course of the planets or stars, the signs or the writing of the heavenly gods, represent the cosmic will . . . the examination undertaken and the decision announced by astral gods and divination priests constitute the act of drawing out and making known that will. And the way of life one leads as a consequence of the decision is the final outcome.[3]

The will of heaven, then, has varying manifestations in the two cultures, but the need to interpret the signs and act on their consequences is common to both.

This study has been an effort to show that in ancient Judaism, methods of interpretation and discourse on the nature of signs were not confined to scripture and its interpretation but extended to the world of celestial, terrestrial, and ritual things and occurrences.

In Context

Most of the sources cited in this study, especially the midrashim and piyyutim, date from the fourth to the sixth centuries. It is precisely these centuries, according to Patricia Cox Miller, that witnessed a "material turn" in polytheistic and Christian philosophy, ritual, and culture from a pattern of denial of the role of the body in pursuing spiritual perfection to a reliance on the physical in aid of the spiritual. Miller describes a shift in values from Plotinus to Iamblichus, the major philosopher of theurgy, and subsequently Proclus, who became known for his treatise on the animation of statues: "The earlier tendency to suppress materiality as fundamental to self-identity was revised when the orienting function of the soul shifted with regard to the spiritual value of the sensible world."[4]

In other words, since Platonism focuses mainly on the purification of the self in uniting with the highest spiritual level, the question was whether the world of bodies and objects was a hindrance or a help. The theurgists sought to prove that this world had an essential role to play. This shift toward a sacramental view of the world—a view, that is, that invests the sensible world with divine presence rather than seeing the sensible as a shadowy reflection of the divine—was already evident in the psychology of Iamblichus, whose views of the soul Proclus largely followed.[5] Iamblichus accordingly developed a theory of theurgy "based on this view of the material world as theophany," in which divine power inhered in "tokens" that could be used in rituals for the reception of divine consciousness.[6] Iamblichus, Proclus, and others of these generations deployed this philosophy in defense of ritual, including sacrifice and divination. In fact, divination experienced renewed attention from intellectuals in the fourth century—both from philosophers like Porphyry and Iamblichus, who searched for theories of its operation, and from Christian theologians like Eusebius, who, for polemical purposes, exploited the pagan philosophers' compunctions.[7] Proclus likewise sought to ground his defense of the animation of statues in the idea that the gods have embedded signification in their instructions for making statues.[8] This idea is a remarkable analogue to the Jewish discourse on the priestly vestments we have seen. In texts from the Palestinian Talmud to the Avodah piyyutim, the vestments are understood as a divinely ordained mode of communication between God and Israel, one that functions on the informational level and on the level of ritual effectiveness as well.

The rabbis and their contemporaries who commented on divination and ritual practices in the fourth century and after were not motivated by the same theological concerns; that is, they apparently did not harbor Platonic aspirations to uniting with the One. Rather, they seem to have stressed the reception and interpretation of the divine word and its fulfillment in law and ritual. Nonetheless, the intellectual atmosphere of the fourth through sixth centuries, in which the inherent meaning of things and their relationship to the spiritual was being reexamined, may well have set in motion concerted thinking among Jews about how the divine will manifested itself in the material world.

If this is true, such thinking was not confined to one sector of Jewish culture in Palestine and Babylonia in late antiquity. Rabbinic midrash includes speculation on the significance of the priestly vestments, a system of signification that was amplified in the Avodah piyyutim. Likewise, the midrashic traditions that portray the Temple and sacrificial system as having been precreated have a higher profile in those piyyutim. While divination traditions are attested in Talmudic stories, we have seen that those stories betray a deep ambivalence about their sanctity and appropriateness. In contrast, we also possess divination texts, no doubt intended for private practitioners, that declare their grounding in hallowed ancestral figures and customs.

These corpora stand at the margins of rabbinic literature. We can thus imagine that the central circles of rabbinic authorities were more likely to hold to the notion of the Torah, as expounded by scholastic tradition, as the exclusive source of revelation. But at the same time, some sectors of Jewish culture in late antiquity subscribed to alternatives to this worldview. Indeed, as we have seen, these alternatives are attested as well in rabbinic literature itself. This suggests that the pantextual theory of revelation was an ideological development in rabbinic thought that shared space with a more encompassing view of divine signification—a view that in turn may have held sway outside rabbinic scholastic circles. To be sure, the Torah's drama of the initial act of creation, by which the creator did things with words, encouraged ancient Jews to see the word as inherently meaningful and powerful. But there existed at the same time a tradition, of ancient vintage, by which the creator also signified to humanity through actions and things.

Notes

CHAPTER 1

1. This designation was first used in the Qur'an (3:110, 4:152) to designate Jews, Christians, and Sabaeans. By the tenth century, Salmon ben Yeruḥim had appropriated the term to designate the Karaites. See Salo W. Baron, *A Social and Religious History of the Jews*, 2nd ed., vol. 5 (New York: Columbia University Press and Philadelphia: Jewish Publication Society, 1957), 236 and 400, n. 31.

2. J. L. Austin, *How to Do Things with Words*, ed. J. O. Urmson and Marina Sbisa (Cambridge, MA: Harvard University Press, 1975). On applications of Austin's ideas to ritual language, see Stanley J. Tambiah, "The Magical Power of Words," *Man* 3 (1968): 177–208; and the references cited in Michael D. Swartz, *Mystical Prayer in Ancient Judaism: An Analysis of Ma`aseh Merkavah* (Tubingen: Mohr, 1992), 1–5.

3. See Lawrence H. Schiffman and Michael D. Swartz, *Hebrew and Aramaic Incantation Texts from the Cairo Genizah: Selected Texts from Taylor-Schechter Box K1* (Sheffield: Sheffield Academic Press, 1992), 42–44. On the problem of multiple languages in ancient Mediterranean magic, see Gideon Bohak, "Hebrew, Hebrew Everywhere? Notes on the Interpretation of Voces Magicae," in *Prayer, Magic, and the Stars in the Ancient and Late Antique World*, ed. Scott Noegel and Brandon Wheeler (University Park: Pennsylvania State University Press, 2003), 69–82. On the multivalence of the use of language in magical texts, see especially David Frankfurter, "The Magic of Writing and the Writing of Magic: The Power of the Word in Egyptian and Greek Traditions," *Helios* 21 (1994): 189–221.

4. On this idea, see Michael D. Swartz, "Judaism and the Idea of Ancient Ritual Theory," in *Jewish Studies at the Crossroads of History: Authority, Diaspora, Tradition*, ed. Ra'anan Boustan, Oren Kosansky, and Marina Rustow (Philadelphia: University of Pennsylvania Press, 2010), 294–317.

5. Francis X. Clooney, S.J., *Thinking Ritually: Rediscovering the Purva Mimamsa of Jaimini* (Vienna: Sammlung de Nobili Institut für Indologie der Universität Wien, 1990). See also Swartz, "Judaism and the Idea of Ancient Ritual Theory."

6. E. Valentine Daniel, *Fluid Signs: Being a Person the Tamil Way* (Berkeley: University of California Press, 1984).

7. Richard J. Parmentier, *The Sacred Remains: Myth, History, and Polity in Belau* (Chicago: University of Chicago Press, 1987); see also William F. Hanks, *Referential Practice: Language and Lived Space among the Maya* (Chicago: University of Chicago Press, 1990).

8. On the ancient history of semiotics, see especially Giovanni Manetti, *Theories of the Sign in Classical Antiquity* (Bloomington: Indiana University Press, 1993); and Peter Struck, *Birth of the Symbol: Ancient Readers at the Limits of Their Texts* (Princeton, NJ: Princeton University Press, 2004).

9. Jacob Brüll, *Doresh le-Ṣiyyon: Kollel Be'urim ve-Tiqunim al ha-Simanim asher ba-Shas* (Vienna: Shlosberg and Bendiner, 1864).

10. On this subject, see Martin S. Jaffee, *Torah in the Mouth: Writing and Oral Tradition in Palestinian Judaism, 200 BCE–400 CE* (New York: Oxford University Press, 2001); on memorization and its cultivation see also Michael D. Swartz, *Scholastic Magic: Ritual and Revelation in Early Jewish Mysticism* (Princeton, NJ: Princeton University Press, 1996).

11. At this point he cites the Talmud, b. Hul. 59–67, which catalogs the anatomical characteristics of animals that are permitted (kosher) under Jewish dietary law (*kashrut*).

12. Here citing b. Niddah 46–48 (see also M. Niddah 5:9), which describes the anatomical indicators of a castrated man (*saris*) and a woman unable to conceive (*aylonit*).

13. Here Brüll cites Moed Qatan 5a; see also M. Moed Qatan 1:2.

14. Heb. *orlah*. On these cases, see also Lev. 19:23–24 and M. Orlah chap. 1.

15. Heb. *ot*. All translations from the Hebrew Bible follow the New Jewish Publication Society translation (NJPS), with occasional modifications, unless otherwise noted.

16. For example, M. Ma'aser Sheni 5:9 and b. Mo'ed Qatan 5a. See also n. 15.

17. José Faur, *Golden Doves with Silver Dots: Semiotics and Textuality in Rabbinic Tradition* (Bloomington: Indiana University Press, 1986), xxii.

18. Ibid., 40.

19. Ibid., xxvii.

20. See especially Susan Handelman, *The Slayers of Moses: The Emergence of Rabbinic Interpretation in Modern Literary Theory* (Albany: SUNY Press, 1982); and Daniel Boyarin, *Intertextuality and the Reading of Midrash* (Bloomington: Indiana University Press, 1990), who argues that Derrida and other postmodern theorists "[make] possible a space for a more sympathetic reading of midrash as an interpretive act" (x).

21. Jacques Derrida, *Of Grammatology* (Baltimore: Johns Hopkins University Press, 1976), 158.

22. Cf. Howard Eilberg-Schwartz, "When the Reader Is in the Write," *Prooftexts* 7 (1987): 199.

23. Handelman, *The Slayers of Moses*.

24. See especially David Stern, "Moses-cide: Midrash and Contemporary Literary Criticism," *Prooftexts* 4 (1984): 15–38.

25. See Eilberg-Schwartz, "When the Reader Is in the Write," 201–2; see also Stern, "Moses-cide," 197; and Boyarin, *Intertextuality*, xii.

26. See chapter 4 and the references cited there.

27. See Manetti, *Theories of the Sign*; and Struck, *Birth of the Symbol*.

28. On Iamblichus as a ritual theorist, see Struck, *Birth of the Symbol*, 204–26.

29. Patricia Cox Miller, *The Corporeal Imagination: Signifying the Holy in Late Ancient Christianity* (Philadelphia: University of Pennsylvania Press, 2009).

30. Cf. Janet Gyatso, "Letter Magic: Peircean Perspective on the Semiotics of Rdo Grub-chen's Dharani Memory," in *In the Mirror of Memory: Reflections on Mindfulness and Remembrance in Indian and Tibetan Buddhism*, ed. Janet Gyatso (Albany: SUNY Press, 1992), 178.

31. See Joseph Yahalom, *Az be-En Kol: Seder ha-'Avodah ha-Ereṣ-Yisraeli ha-Qadum le-Yom ha-Kippurim* (Jerusalem: Magnes, 1996), 52–53; Michael D. Swartz, "Ritual about Myth about Ritual: Toward an Understanding of the *Avodah* in the Rabbinic Period," *Journal of Jewish Thought and Philosophy* 6 (1997): 135–55; Swartz, "Judaism and the Idea

of Ancient Ritual Theory"; and Michael D. Swartz, "Chains of Tradition from Avot to the Avodah Piyyutim," in *Judaism, Christianity, and the Roman Empire*, ed. Natalie Dohrman and Annette Yoshiko Reed (Philadelphia: University of Pennsylvania Press, forthcoming).

32. See Henry Louis Gates, *The Signifying Monkey: A Theory of Afro-American Literary Criticism* (New York: Oxford University Press, 1988), 3–22.

33. See ibid., 23–43.

34. See ibid., 44–88, especially Gates's cataloging of forms of signifying that use language in ways other than to convey meaning (68–69).

35. See especially Steven Fine, *Art and Judaism in the Greco-Roman World: Toward a New Jewish Archaeology* (Cambridge: Cambridge University Press, 2005); Kalman P. Bland, *The Artless Jew: Medieval and Modern Affirmations and Denials of the Visual* (Princeton, NJ: Princeton: Princeton University Press, 2000); and Margaret Olin, *The Nation without Art: Examining Modern Discourses on Jewish Art* (Lincoln: University of Nebraska Press, 2001).

36. Bland, *The Artless Jew*, 3–12.

37. Zvi I. Abusch, "*Alaktu* and *Halakhah*: Oracular Decision, Divine Revelation," *Harvard Theological Review* 80 (1987): 15–42.

38. See chapter 4.

39. Howard Eilberg-Schwartz, ed., *People of the Body: Jews and Judaism from an Embodied Perspective* (Albany: SUNY Press, 1992). As Edith Wyschogrod points out, two streams of postmodern thought, pantextuality and corporeality, have often operated independently of each other. See Edith Wyschogrod, "Towards a Postmodern Ethics: Corporeality and Alterity," in *The Ethical*, ed. Edith Wyschogrod and Gerald P. McKenny (Malden, MA: Blackwell, 2003), 54–65.

CHAPTER 2

1. M. Avot 5:6; for details, see chap. 5.

2. For this line of reasoning, see Tosefta Eruvin 8:23, ed. Saul Lieberman (New York: Jewish Theological Seminary, 1962–88), 138, and Hagigah 1:9 (p. 379). For additional lists of things created at twilight, see, for example, *Mekhilta de-Rabbi Ishmael*, ed. H. S. Horovitz and I. A. Rabin (Jerusalem: Wahrman, 1970), *Beshallaḥ Vayisa*, chap. 5, p. 171; *Sifre 'al Sefer Devarim Zot ha-Berakhah* 355, ed. Louis Finkelstein (New York: Jewish Theological Seminary of America, 1969), 418; Avot de-Rabbi Natan B, chap. 37, ed. S. Schechter (London, 1887), 95; Jerusalem Targum Num. 22:28; *Pirqe de-Rabbi Eliezer*, chap. 19 (Warsaw, 1852; repr. Jerusalem, 1990), fol. 45a. On the sources, see Louis Ginzberg, *Legends of the Jews* (Philadelphia: Jewish Publication Society, 1947), 5:109, n. 99.

3. On the place of myth in Jewish historiography, see S. Daniel Breslauer, ed., *The Seductiveness of Jewish Myth: Challenge or Response?* (Albany: SUNY Press, 1997), especially Breslauer's introduction, 1–10; and Steven M. Wasserstrom, "A Rustling in the Woods: The Turn to Myth in Weimar Jewish Thought," in Breslauer, *The Seductiveness of Jewish Myth*, 97–122.

4. For the most comprehensive recent statement, see Michael Fishbane, *Biblical Myth and Rabbinic Mythmaking* (Oxford: Oxford University Press, 2003); see also Maren R. Niehoff, "The Phoenix in Rabbinic Literature," *Harvard Theological Review* 89 (1996): 245–65; Jeffrey L. Rubenstein, "From Mythic Motifs to Sustained Myth: The Revision of Rabbinic Traditions in Medieval Midrashim," *Harvard Theological Review* 89 (1996): 131–59; and Yehudah Liebes, *Studies in Jewish Myth and Jewish Messianism* (Albany: SUNY Press, 1993).

5. See Niehoff, "The Phoenix in Rabbinic Literature," 247.

6. Fishbane, *Biblical Myth*.

7. Rubenstein, "Mythic Motifs," 134, citing Mircea Eliade, *The Sacred and the Profane: The Nature of Religion* (New York: Harper & Row, 1961); and Mircea Eliade, *Myth and Reality* (New York: Harper & Row, 1963).

8. Heb. *dipteraòt*, a document made from hide; see Marcus Jastrow, *Dictionary of the Targumim, the Talmud Babli and Yerushalmi, and the Midrashic Literature* (New York: Judaica Press, 1975).

9. Genesis Rabbah 1:1, ed. J. Theodor and C. Albeck, *Midrash Bereshit Rabbah*, 2nd ed. (Jerusalem: Wahrman, 1965), 1–2. This idea is also implied in M. Avot 3:14: "Beloved is Israel, for they are given a precious treasure by which the world was created, as it is said, 'For I give you a good instruction; do not forsake My Torah' (Prov 4:2)."

10. Wisdom of Solomon 7:25–26; the translation is from David Winston, *The Wisdom of Solomon: A New Translation with Introduction and Commentary* (Garden City, NY: Doubleday, Anchor Bible, 1979), 184; see his notes there.

11. The literature on the logos in Philo is substantial; see, for example, David Winston, *Logos and Mystical Theology in Philo of Alexandria* (Cincinnati: Hebrew Union College Press, 1985). On the possible relationship of Philo's concept to R. Hoshaya's statement, see Winston, *Logos and Mystical Theology*, 25; cf. Jakob Freudenthal, *Hellenistische Studien*, Jahresbericht des jüdisch-theologischen Seminars, 1874, vol. 1, p. 73; W. Bacher, "The Church Father, Origen, and Rabbi Hoshaya," *Jewish Quarterly Review* 3 (1891): 357–60; cf. also A. Marmorstein, "Philo and the Names of God," *Jewish Quarterly Review* 12 (1932): 295–306; and Alan F. Segal and N. A. Dahl, "Philo and the Rabbis on the Names of God," *Journal for the Study of Judaism* 9 (1978): 1–28. Maren Niehoff argues that Philo derives his peculiarly central concept of the Logos not from Middle Platonism but from internal Jewish exegetical dynamics; see Maren R. Niehoff, *Philo on Jewish Identity and Culture* (Tubingen: Mohr Siebeck, 2001). Daniel Boyarin sees in the concept evidence for a pervasive Jewish binitarian conception of God; see Daniel Boyarin, *Border Lines: The Partition of Judaeo-Christianity* (Philadelphia: University of Pennsylvania Press, 2004), 112–27.

12. M. Avot 5:22.

13. On precreation and emanation in Midrash and related sources, see Ginzberg, *Legends of the Jews*, 5:3–16. Ginzberg evidently planned an excursus on precreation but it never appeared (5:3).

14. See Ginzberg, *Legends of the Jews*, 5:109, n. 99.

15. For lists of sources, see, for example, Theodor and Albeck, *Bereshit Rabbah*, 6; Finkelstein, *Sifre Devarim*, 70; *Midrash Tanḥuma*, ed. S. Buber (Vilna, 1885; repr. Jerusalem, 1960), Bemidbar, 34–35; and *Midrash Tehillim*, ed. S. Buber (Vilna 1891; repr. Jerusalem, 1965), 391–92; and esp. Yehoshua Granat, "'Az mi-Lifne Bereshit:' Devarim She-Qadmu le-Veri'at ha-Olam: Mesorot ve-Darkhe 'Iṣuvan ba-Piyyut ha-Qadum 'al Reqa Meqorotav" (PhD diss.; Hebrew University of Jerusalem, 2009, reprinted and amended, 2009). On the lists of things created on the sixth day, see the analysis by Anthony J. Saldarini, *The Fathers According to Rabbi Nathan* (*Aboth de Rabbi Nathan*) *Version B* (Leiden: Brill, 1975), 306–10. Cf. also the list of things created on the first day in Jubilees 2.2.

16. Finkelstein, *Sifre Devarim*, 70.

17. Theodor and Albeck, *Midrash Bereshit Rabbah*, 6.

18. Tanḥuma Buber, Bemidbar, 34–35.

19. *Midrash Tanḥuma* (Warsaw, n.d.), vol. 2, pp. 51–52.

20. Buber, *Midrash Tehillim* 72:6 (pp. 326–27), 90:12 (p. 391), and 93:3 (p. 414).

21. Burton L. Visotzky, *Midrash Mishle* (New York: Jewish Theological Seminary of America, 1990), 59.

22. *Pirqe Rabbi Eliezer* (Warsaw, 1852; repr. Jerusalem, 1990), fols. 5a–9a.

23. M. Friedman (Ish-Shalom), *Seder Eliyahu Rabbah ve-Seder Eliyahu Zuta (Tana de-ve Eliyahu)*, 3rd ed. (Jerusalem: Wahrmann, 1969), 160–61.

24. See H. L. Strack and Günter Stemberger, *Introduction to the Talmud and Midrash* (Minneapolis: Fortress Press, 1996), 296–98.

25. On the complex history of the Tanḥuma-Yelamedenu, see Marc Bregman, *Sifrut Tanḥuma-Yelamdenu: Te'ur Nusaḥeha ve-'Iyunim be-Darkhe Hithavutam* (Piscataway, NJ: Gorgias, 2003).

26. While *Pirqe de-Rabbi Eliezer* includes the list as part of an integrated homily, the items in the list themselves are not brought together to form a complete picture, as they are in *Midrash Tehillim*.

27. Granat, "'Az Mi-lifne Bereshit.'"

28. The Babylonian Talmud identifies the tradition as a *beraita*, that is, from tannaitic Palestine. Granat, however, concludes that even if the *beraita* originally was Palestinian, it was not accepted in this form in tannaitic and amoraic Palestine ("'Az Mi-lifne Bereshit,'" 75).

29. Granat, "'Az-Mi-lifne Bereshit,'" 72–82.

30. *Avot de-Rabbi Natan*, chap. 27, ed. Schechter, p 95. Cf. also *Pirqe de-Rabbi Eliezer*, chap. 3, which does not specify when God conceived of those ten things. For this, see the commentary by David Luria (Radal) in this source. On these sources, see Granat, "'Az Mi-lifne Bereshit,'" 81.

31. Heb. *she-'alu ba-maḥshavah le-hibarot*.

32. The New Jewish Publication Society (NJPS) translates, "Your fathers seemed to me like the first fig to ripen on a fig tree"; cf. NJPS's critical note to that verse.

33. Heb. *marom me-rishon*, literally, "from the first."

34. The NJPS translates, "While the sun lasts, may his name endure." *Lifne shemesh*, lit., "before the sun," is taken here to mean that the name of the messiah was established before the sun was created.

35. Genesis Rabbah 1:4, ed. Theodor and Albeck, p. 6.

36. Heb. *Maqom*.

37. *Sifre Devarim Eqev*, chap. 37, ed. Finkelstein, p. 70.

38. In the manuscripts of Sifre, this gloss appears in the unit quoted here; however, it also appears in the following unit as another discourse (*davar aḥer*). Therefore Finkelstein suggests that the gloss was extraneous to the original text of the unit. See Finkelstein's note.

39. See Martin Buber and Franz Rosenzweig, *Scripture and Translation*, trans. Lawrence Rosenwald with Everett Fox (Bloomington: Indiana University Press, 1994), 138; Umberto Cassuto, *Commentary on the Book of Exodus* (Jerusalem: Magnes, 1967), chaps. 39–40; Moshe Weinfeld, "Sabbath, Temple, and the Enthronement of the Lord—The Problem of the Sitz im Leben of Genesis 1:1–2:3," in *Mélanges biblique et orientales en l'honeur de M. Henri Cazelles* (Neukirchen Vluyn: Butzon and Berker Kevelaer, 1981), 501–12.

40. Weinfeld, "Sabbath."

41. On this cluster of concepts, see especially Jon D. Levenson, *Sinai and Zion: An Entry into the Jewish Bible* (Minneapolis: Winston Press, 1985), 138–42.

42. For the idea that David's pattern for the Temple is based on the heavenly prototype, see Wisdom of Solomon 9:8; on the general idea of the heavenly Temple, see A. Aptowitzer, "*Bet ha-Miqdash shel Ma`alah `al Pi ha-`Aggadah,*" *Tarbiz* 2 (1931): 137–53, 257–87.

43. Tanḥuma Buber Naso 19.

44. Heb. *mi-qedem* usually taken to mean "in the East."

45. Heb. *hekhal kis'i.*

46. Genesis Rabbah 1:4, ed. Theodor and Albeck, p. 7.

47. On the Avodah in late antiquity, see Michael D. Swartz and Joseph Yahalom, *Avodah: Ancient Poems for Yom Kippur* (University Park: Pennsylvania State University Press, 2005) and the bibliography there; all translations and line numbers of Avodah piyyutim here are from this volume. See also J. Elbogen, *Studien zur Geschichte des jüdischen Gottesdienstes* (Berlin: Mayer & Miller, 1907); Zvi Malachi, "Ha-'Avodah' le-Yom ha-Kippurim—'Ofiyah, Toledoteha ve-Hitpathuta ba-Shirah ha-'Ivrit" (PhD diss., Hebrew University, 1974); E. Daniel Goldschmidt, ed., *Maḥazor le-Yamim Nora'im (Ashkenaz)* (Jerusalem: Mosad Bialik, 1970), 1: 18–25 of the introduction; Aaron Mirsky, *Piyyute Yose ben Yose*, 2nd ed. (Jerusalem: Mosad Bialik, 1991); and Yahalom, *Az be-En Kol.*

48. "Azkir Gevurot," line 10; Swartz and Yahalom, *Avodah*, 224–25.

49. God.

50. "Aromem la-El," lines 125–28, Yahalom, *Az be-En Kol*, 165. For the following argument, see also Yahalom, *Az be-En Kol*, 51–52; and Swartz and Yaholom, *Avodah*, 33–34.

51. See Ephraim Urbach, "Seride Tanḥuma-Yelamedenu," *Qoveṣ `al Yad* 6 (1966): 12.

52. Lines 738–39; Swartz and Yahalom, *Avodah*, 201.

53. See T. Kip. 2:14.

54. Lines 35–36 and 53–72; Swartz and Yahalom, *Avodah*, 106–11.

55. Heb. *Tohu va-Vohu.*

56. Lines 34–36; referring apparently to the primordial waters, on which the rafters of heaven rest.

57. The preposition *be-* beginning each stanza is translated in this section as "by" or "with," according to the structure outlined earlier.

58. Lines 37–38.

59. B. Shab 99a.

60. According to y. Hag 2:1; and Genesis Rabbah 10:3, ed. Theodor and Albeck, p. 75, snow was used to create the world.

61. Lines 45–46, alluding to Job 38:23.

62. Lines 57–58.

63. Lines 65–66.

64. That is, God himself.

65. Lines 31–32; Swartz and Yahalom, *Avodah*, 230–31.

66. Lines 33–36.

67. On this piyyut, see Swartz and Yahalom, *Avodah*, 291–341; Elbogen, *Studien*, 79–81; and Malachi, "Ha-'Avodah,'" 20–22.

68. That is, for Israel.

69. Fish that are ritually pure.

70. See Isa. 27:1. Here the poet is referring to the Leviathan.

71. The rhetorical question is placed here for the sake of the acrostic; the first line in the stanza (line 19) begins *Ha-lo'*.

72. Heb. *hikhsharta*; that is, "You made the Behemoth kosher."

73. Heb. *va-tishqod*.

74. Lines 20–22, Swartz and Yahalom, *Avodah*, 296–97.

75. Line 19: *hitvita*; see Mirsky's note to this line, *Piyyute Yose ben Yose*, 175.

76. Line 20: *Hoda'ta simane ma'akhal le-taharah*.

77. See Mirsky, *Piyyute Yose ben Yose*, 222–39.

78. That is, God placed signs in those animals that are permitted (kosher) to Jews.

79. Line 18, Mirsky, *Piyyute Yose ben Yose*, 224. That is, the other nations of the world were given all edible animals; see Genesis 9:3.

CHAPTER 3

1. See Jonathan Z. Smith, "The Bare Facts of Ritual," in his *Imagining Religion: From Babylon to Jonestown* (Chicago: University of Chicago Press, 1982), 53–65.

2. Catherine Bell, *Ritual Theory, Ritual Practice* (New York: Oxford University Press, 1992), 108–10, 114–17; and Pierre Bourdieu, *Outline of a Theory of Practice* (Cambridge: Cambridge University Press, 1977), 171–83.

3. See Michael D. Swartz, "Judaism and the Idea of Ancient Ritual Theory," in *Jewish Studies at the Crossroads of History: Authority, Diaspora, Tradition*, ed. Ra'anan Boustan, Oren Kosansky, and Marina Rustow (Philadelphia: University of Pennsylvania Press, 2010), 294–317.

4. Roland Barthes, *The Fashion System*, trans. Matthew Ward and Richard Howard (New York: Hill & Wang, 1983), 27 (italics in the original).

5. Ant. 15.403–8.

6. A. Leo Oppenheim, "Golden Garments of the Gods," *Journal of Near Eastern Studies* 8 (1949): 172–93.

7. Ibid., 191.

8. Ibid.

9. Lynda L. Coon, *Sacred Fictions: Holy Women and Hagiography in Late Antiquity* (Philadelphia: University of Pennsylvania Press), 53. On the tension between the Western vestments, which approximated more closely those of the biblical priesthood, and the more ascetic dress of the Eastern churches, see pp. 63–64.

10. On early rabbinic attitudes to sacrifice, see Jacob Neusner, "Map without Territory: The Mishnah's System of Sacrifice," *History of Religions* 19 (1979): 103–27. On theories of sacrifice in liturgical poetry and the contrast between the two approaches, see Swartz, "Judaism and the Idea of Ancient Ritual Theory"; and Michael D. Swartz, "Sage, Priest, and Poet: Typologies of Leadership in the Ancient Synagogue," in *Jews, Christians and Polytheists in the Ancient Synagogue: Cultural Interaction During the Greco-Roman Period*, ed. Steven Fine (London: Routledge, 1999), 101–17.

11. For an analysis of the biblical sources on the vestments, see Menahem Haran, *Temples and Temple Service in Ancient Israel: An Inquiry into the Character of Cult Phenomena and the Historical Setting of the Priestly School* (Oxford: Clarendon Press, 1978),

165–74. For commentaries to Exodus 28 and 39, see also Nahum Sarna's commentary to those chapters in *Exodus: The Traditional Hebrew Text with the New JPS Translation: Commentary by Nahum M. Sarna* (Philadelphia: Jewish Publication Society, 1991), 177–86, 232–35.

12. This translation of terms for the vestments is based on the New Jewish Publication Society (NJPS), slightly modified. Explanatory notes are placed in parentheses.

13. On Second Temple depictions of the vestments, see Douglas R. Edwards, "The Social, Religious, and Political Aspects of Costume in Josephus," in *The World of Roman Costume*, ed. Judith Lynn Sebesta and Larissa Bonfante (Madison: University of Wisconsin Press, 1994), 156–57; and Alfred Rubens, *History of Jewish Costume*, 2nd ed. (London: Peter Owen, 1981), 12–16. On Jewish dress in general in late antiquity, see Lucille A. Roussin, "Costume in Roman Palestine: Archaeological Remains and the Evidence from the Mishnah," in *The World of Roman Costume*, ed. Judith Lynn Sebesta and Larissa Bonfante (Madison: University of Wisconsin Press, 1994), 182–90.

14. See *m. Yoma* 7:3–4 and *y. Yoma* 7:3–5 (44b).

15. See Sir. 45:12 and Josephus *Ant.* 3.172–78; see especially Ralph Marcus's commentary in LCL.

16. See, for example, *b. B. Qam.* 94b; cf. Yeruḥam b. Meshulam's fourteenth-century code *Toledot Adam ve-Ḥavah* (Venice, 1553), fol. 26b, in which the *avnet* has the ancillary function of preventing lewd thoughts during prayer. Cf. Uri Ehrlich, *The Nonverbal Language of Prayer: A New Approach to Jewish Liturgy* (Tubingen: Mohr, 2004), 136–38.

17. Moshe Levine, *The Tabernacle: Its Structure and Utensils* (Tel Aviv: Melechet Hamishkan; London: Soncino Press, 1969).

18. Rubens, *History of Jewish Costume*, 14–15.

19. See, for example, Yisrael Ariel, ed., *Maḥzor ha-Miqdash: Nosaḥ Ashkenaz* (Jerusalem: Mekhon ha-Miqdash, 1996).

20. See C. H. Kraeling, *The Excavations at Dura Europos: The Synagogue* (final report, vol. 8, part 1) (1956; repr. New York: Ktav, 1979), 126–28.

21. On the synagogue and its mosaic, see Zeev Weiss, *The Sepphoris Synagogue: Deciphering an Ancient Message through Its Archaeological and Socio-Historical Contexts* (Jerusalem: Israel Exploration Society, Institute of Archaeology, Hebrew University of Jerusalem, 2005); and Zeev Weiss and Ehud Netzer, *Promise and Redemption: A Synagogue Mosaic from Sepphoris* (Jerusalem: Israel Museum, 1996). For another interpretation of the mosaic and its function in the context of the synagogue, see Steven Fine, "Art and the Liturgical Context of the Sepphoris Synagogue Mosaic," in *Galilee through the Centuries: Confluence of Cultures*, ed. Eric M. Meyers (Winona Lake, IN: Eisenbrauns, 1999), 227–37.

22. This detail of the vestments, which is significant in several interpretative schemes, is discussed later in this chapter.

23. See Weiss, *The Sepphoris Synagogue*, 152; Weiss and Netzer, *Promise and Redemption*, 20.

24. Josephus, *Ant.* 3.151–78 and *Bell.* 5.227–36; *Ep. Arist.* 96–99; Philo, *Vita Mosis* 2.109–35; *Spec. Leg.* 1.82–97.

25. See, for example, Mirsky, *Piyyute Yose ben Yose*, 160; and Joseph Yahalom, *Az be-En Kol*, 126.

26. For the example of the gems on the breastpiece in Second Temple sources, see Robert Hayward, "Pseudo-Philo and the Priestly Oracle," *Journal of Jewish Studies* 46 (1995): 48–54.

27. See C. T. R. Hayward, *The Jewish Temple: A Non-Biblical Sourcebook* (London: Routledge, 1996), 45–47.

28. Jub. 3:26–27. See Hayward, *The Jewish Temple*, 90.

29. Hayward, *The Jewish Temple*, 45. The scholarship on the garments of Adam and Eve in Jewish and Christian interpretation is considerable. For recent analyses and bibliography, see Gary Anderson, "The Garments of Skin in Apocryphal Narrative and Biblical Commentary," in *Studies in Ancient Midrash*, ed. James L. Kugel (Cambridge, MA: Harvard University Center for Jewish Studies, 2001), 101–43; and Alexander Toepel, "When Did Adam Wear the Garments of Light?" *Journal of Jewish Studies* 61 (2010): 62–71; see also Jonathan Z. Smith, "The Garments of Shame," *Human Resources* 5 (1966): 217–38; and Sebastian P. Brock, "Clothing Metaphors as a Means of Theological Expression in Syriac Tradition," in *Typus, Symbol, Allegorie bei den östlichen Vätern und ihren Parallelen im Mittelalter*, ed. Margot Schmidt and Carl Friedrich Geyer (Regensburg: Pustet, 1982), 11–40.

30. Gk. *galaktinon*.

31. Genesis Rabbah 1:1, ed. Theodor and Albeck, 1–2, and 20:12, 196–97.

32. Tanḥ. Buber *Toledot* 12.

33. See ibid., 4.

34. Heb. *bamot*. On the permitting of the high places, cf. b. Zeb. 112b and b. Meg. 10a.

35. Heb. *Avodah*.

36. Cf. b. Zeb. 112b.

37. Tanḥ. Buber *Toledot* 12.

38. Henry Fischel, "The Use of Sorites (*Climax, Gradatio*) in the Tannaitic Period," *Hebrew Union College Annual* 44 (1973): 119–51; Anthony Saldarini, *Scholastic Rabbinism: A Literary Study of the Fathers According to Rabbi Nathan* (Chico, CA: Scholars Press, 1982); and Abram Tropper, *Wisdom Politics, and Historiography: Tractate Avot in the Context of the Graeco-Roman Near East* (Oxford: Oxford University Press, 2004). On the uses of the sorites in the literature of early Jewish mysticism and magic, see Swartz, *Scholastic Magic*, 173–205. On chains of tradition in piyyut, see Swartz, "Chains of Tradition."

39. Fischel, "Sorites," 124–26. Cf. Isaac Heinemann, *Darkhe ha-Aggadah* (Jerusalem: Magnes and Masada, 1970), 30; and Swartz, *Scholastic Magic*, 197–98.

40. In another midrash, Genesis Rabbah 63:13, ed. Theodor and Albeck, 697, the cloak has the power to attract animals and is stolen by Nimrod and passed down to Esau. See Heinemann, *Darkhe ha-Aggadah*, 30.

41. *Sifra Mekhilta de-Millu'im* 1:11, ed. I. H. Weiss (Vienna: Ya'akov ha-Kohen Shlosberg,, 1862), 1:6 (fol. 41a), to Lev. 8:1–13: *Mekhilta de-Millu'im* is a fragment of a composition related to *Sifra*, which was inserted into some *Sifra* manuscripts and editions. See H. L. Strack and G. Stemberger, *Introduction to the Talmud and Midrash* (Edinburgh: T&T Clark, 1991), 259–66. Cf. also the text in *Sifra or Torat Kohanim according to Codex Assemani LXVI with a Hebrew Introduction by Louis Finkelstein* (New York: Jewish Theological Seminary of America, 1956), 179–98. This translation is based on the text in *Codex Assemani*, 180.

42. See the commentary of Ra'abad.

43. Josephus, *Ant.* 2.215–17; see Edwards, "The Social, Religious, and Political Aspects of Costume in Josephus," 156.

44. On the gemological tradition, see Joshua Trachtenberg, *Jewish Magic and Superstition: A Study in Folk Religion* (1939; repr. New York: Atheneum, 1982), 136–38; the excerpt from *Sefer Gematriot* printed on pp. 165–68; and Moritz Steinschneider, "Lapidarien, ein culturgeschightlicher Versuch," in *Semitic Studies in Memory of Rev. Dr. Alexander Kohut*, ed. George Alexander Kohut (Berlin: S. Calvary, 1897), 42–72.

45. See Bahya b. Asher, commentary to Exodus 28:15–20 and Genesis 49, *Rabbenu Bahyah: Bi'ur 'al ha-Torah*, ed. Shimon Shevel (Jerusalem: Mosad ha-Rav Kook, 1966–67), 1:378–95 and 2:296–302. See also Abraham Portaleone, *Shilte ha-Gibborim* (Jerusalem, 1970), chaps. 46–50 (fols. 44a–51a). My thanks to Adam Shear for the latter reference.

46. Philo, *Vita Mosis* 2.23–26.

47. Hayward, *The Jewish Temple.*

48. The translation used here is that of David Winston, *The Wisdom of Solomon: A New Translation with Introduction and Commentary* (Garden City, NY: Doubleday, Anchor Bible, 1979), 314. Cf. Yahalom, *Az be-'En Kol*, 32.

49. *Quaest. in Ex.* 2.112.

50. Naomi G. Cohen, "The Elucidation of Philo's *Spec. Leg.* 4.137–38: 'Stamped Too with Genuine Seals," in *Classical Studies in Honor of David Sohlberg*, ed. Ranon Katzoff, Yaakov, and David Schaps (Ramat Gan: Bar-Ilan University Press, 1996), 153–66.

51. H. C. Kee, "Testaments of the Twelve Patriarchs," in *The Old Testament Pseudepigrapha*, ed. James H. Charlesworth (Garden City, NY: Doubleday, 1983), 1:790–91.

52. The translation is that of Patrick W. Shekhan and Alexander A. Di Lella, *The Wisdom of Ben Sira* (New York: Doubleday, Anchor Bible, 1987), 507.

53. See Leviticus Rabbah, ed. Mordecai Margulies, *Midrash Vayiqra Rabbah* (New York: Jewish Theological Seminary of America, 1993), 210–12; Jacob Mann, *The Bible as Read and Preached in the Old Synagogue* (1940; repr. New York: Ktav, 1971), vol. 1, p. 258, in the Hebrew section; see also Cant. R. 4:5.

54. B. Zeb. 88b; b. Arak. 16a.

55. Hannaniah, *Haverehon de-Rabbaban*, one of two lay brothers who made their living as shoemakers and studied with R. Yohanan in Tiberius.

56. B. Zeb. 88b.

57. Y. Yoma 7:3 (44b–c).

58. The idea here seems to be that Joseph's tunic was made from a mix of wool and flax, forbidden according to Deuteronomy 22:11. See Margulies, *Vayiqra Rabbah*, 210, and the sources cited in his commentary.

59. This passage appears in a gloss in MS. Leiden and was incorporated into the Venice and the other editions.

60. This phrase appears in a gloss in MS. Leiden.

61. So Jastrow, *Dictionary*, s.v. 'qm.

62. See Rashi's comment to b. Zeb. 88b, which he cites as a tradition regarding b. Arak. 16a: "The sin of teraphim is revealed; if there is an ephod there are no teraphim."

63. On the valorization of the high priest in the Avodah piyyutim, see Michael D. Swartz and Joseph Yahalom, *Avodah*; Swartz, "Sage, Priest, and Poet"; Swartz, "Judaism and the Idea of Ritual Theory"; and Swartz, "Chains of Tradition."

64. Heb., *kefulah meshubṣset*. According to some sources, such as y. Yoma 3:6 (40c) and Ben Sira 45:12–13, it was a double garment. Conversely, according to *Sifra Ṣav* chap. 2, and b. Yoma 72b, the term *shesh*, translated here as "fine linen," means that it was made of six-strand thread. On the possible interpretations of this line, see Mirsky's commentary, *Piyyute Yose ben Yose*, 155.

65. Line 159.

66. Lines 551–52.

67. That is, Joseph.

68. Line 160.

69. Verbally, through slander.

70. Line 168.

71. Lines 559–60.

72. On this idea, see the classic essay by Solomon Schechter, "The *Zachuth* of the Fathers," in *Aspects of Rabbinic Theology*, ed. Solomon Schechter, 2nd ed. (New York: Schocken Books, 1961), 170–98.

73. Shekhan and Di Lella, *The Wisdom of Ben Sira*, 506–7.

74. Referring to Aaron; see n. 75.

75. Although this is a reference to Isaiah 40:3, Yahalom also suggests a relationship to Aaron's intervention in Numbers 17 (*Az be-'En Kol*, 32).

76. Heb. *Shekhinah*.

77. Lines 567–70; see Isa. 59:17.

78. See Gershom Scholem, *Major Trends in Jewish Mysticism*, 2nd ed. (New York: Schocken Books, 1954), 40–79; David Halperin, *The Faces of the Chariot: Early Jewish Responses to Ezekiel's Vision* (Tubingen: Mohr, 1988); and Peter Schäfer, *The Hidden and Manifest God: Some Major Themes in Early Jewish Mysticism* (Albany: SUNY Press, 1992). On affinities to Temple literature, see Johann Meier, *Vom Kultus zum Gnosis* (Salzburg: Otto Müller, 1964); Martha Himmelfarb, *Ascent to Heaven in Jewish and Christian Apocalypses* (Oxford: Oxford University Press, 1993); Swartz, *Scholastic Magic*, 169–72; and Rachel Elior, *The Three Temples: On the Emergence of Jewish Mysticism* (Oxford: Littman Library of Jewish Civilization, 2004).

79. Leviticus Rabbah 21:12, ed. Margulies, 492–93. Cf. *y. Yoma* 5:3 (42c), *t. Sota* 13:5, *b. Yoma* 39b, and *b. Men* 109b. The idea that the priest is a visitor in the divine abode who effectively impersonates angels recalls similar ideas in Hekhalot literature; cf. Swartz, *Scholastic Magic*, 168.

80. On dress as the distinguishing characteristic of gods and priests, cf. Oppenheim, "Golden Garments of the Gods."

81. Lines 1–4 of "Emet Mah Nehedar" ("Truly, How Glorious"), a version of which is published in E. Daniel Goldschmidt, ed., *Maḥazor*, 2: 483–84; and Swartz and Yahalom, *Avodah*, 343–47. For the poem in Ben Sira, see M. H. Segal, *Sefer Ben Sira ha-Shalem* (Jerusalem: Mosad Bialik, 1972), 240–46. On the hymn, see Cecil Roth, "Ecclesiasticus in the Synagogue Service," *Journal of Biblical Literature* 71 (1952): 171–78.

82. Mirsky, *Piyyute Yose ben Yose*, 192.

83. The conjunction *vav* is used here for the acrostic.

84. That is, the Tetragrammaton, for which *YY* is a common scribal circumlocution.

85. Lines 645–46, 651–56.

86. See, for example, *Vita Mosis* 2.133–35.

87. Edmund Leach, "The Logic of Sacrifice," in his *Culture and Communication* (Cambridge: Cambridge University Press, 1976), 81–93; and H. Hubert and M. Mauss, *Sacrifice: Its Nature and Function* (Chicago: University of Chicago Press, 1964).

CHAPTER 4

1. On the extent of the influence of Hinduism, Buddhism, and Daoism on Cage's thought and composition, see David Patterson, "Cage and Asia: History and Sources," in *The Cambridge Companion to John Cage*, ed. David Nicholls (Cambridge: Cambridge University Press, 2002), 41–60.

2. This paraphrase is my own recollection of the interview, which I heard on the radio in New York. My thanks to Andy Lanset, Tim Page, John Bewley, Chris Villars, Sebastian Calren, and Steven Swartz, who helped me in my (unfortunately unsuccessful) attempt to track down a transcript of the interview.

3. The phrase is originally from Comte de Lautréamont's *Les chants de Maldoror*, canto 6; see Alexis Lykiard, trans., *Maldoror & the Complete Works of the Comte de Lautréamont* (Cambridge: Exact Change, 1994), 193. For a compilation of strategies used by the Dadaists and Surrealists, see Emmanuel Garrigues, ed., *Les jeux surrealists: Mars 1921–septembre 1962* (n.p.; Gallimard, 1995); and Alastair Brotchie, *A Book of Surrealist Games* (Boston: Shambhalah Redstone Editions, 1995).

4. On random number generation, see Deborah J. Bennet, *Randomness* (Cambridge, MA: Harvard University Press, 1998), 132–51.

5. On the history of chance operations, see Bennett, *Randomness*, 11–45.

6. See, for example, Daniel Matt, *Zohar: The Book of Enlightenment* (New York: Paulist Press, 1983), 27–29; Gershom Scholem, *Kabbalah* (Jerusalem: Keter, 1974), 188; and, more comprehensively, Amos Goldreich, *Shem ha-Kotev u-Khetivah Otomatit be-Sifrut ha-Zohar u-va-Modernizem* (Los Angeles: Cherub Press, 2010), which also deals extensively with the modern history of the idea of automatism.

7. Max Ernst, *Beyond Painting, and Other Writings by the Artist and His Friends* (New York: Wittenborn, Schultz, 1948).

8. Walter Benjamin, "Surrealism: The Last Snapshot of the European Intelligentsia," in *Selected Writings*, ed. Marcus Bullock and Michael W. Jennings (Cambridge, MA: Belknap Press of Harvard University Press, 1996), 208.

9. Ibid.

10. See Jonathan Z. Smith, "Sacred Persistence: Towards a Redescription of Canon," in his *Imagining Religion: From Babylon to Jonestown* (Chicago: University of Chicago Press, 1982), 36–52; Struck, *Birth of the Symbol*; and see also chapter 1 in this book.

11. Manetti, *Theories of the Sign*.

12. Eric Leichtz, "The Origins of Scholarship," in *Die Rolle der Astronomie in den Kulturen Mesopotamiens: Beiträge zum 3. Grazer Morgenländischen Symposion (23-27 September 1991)*, ed. Hannes D. Galter (Graz: GrazKult, 1993), 21–29.

13. See Saul Lieberman, *Hellenism in Jewish Palestine* (New York: Jewish Theological Seminary of America, 1962), 70–78; Michael Fishbane, "The Qumran Pesher and Traits of Ancient Hermeneutics," *Proceedings of the Sixth World Congress of Jewish Studies* 1 (1975): 97–114; and Jeffrey H. Tigay, "An Early Technique of Aggadic Exegesis," in *History, Histo-*

riography, and Interpretation, ed. H. Tadmor and M. Weinfeld (Jerusalem: Magnes, 1984), 169–89.

14. For ancient Greece, where divination was institutionalized as well as domesticated, see Sarah Isles Johnston, *Ancient Greek Divination* (Malden, MA: Wiley-Blackwell, 2008); for ancient Israel and its neighbors, see Ann Jeffers, *Magic and Divination in Ancient Palestine and Syria* (Leiden: Brill, 1996).; and Frederick H. Cryer, *Divination in Ancient Israel and Its Near Eastern Environment: A Socio-Historical Investigation* (Sheffield: Sheffield Academic Press, 1994).

15. On the Babylonian liver models, see A. Leo Oppenheim, *Ancient Mesopotamia: Portrait of a Dead Civilization* (Chicago: University of Chicago Press, 1964), 215–16; and Jan-Waalke Meyer, *Untersuchungen zu den Tonlebermodellen aus dem AltenOrient* (Kevelaer: Butzon und Bercker; Neukirchen-Vluyn: Neukirchener Verlag, 1987). On an Etruscan bronze liver model, see L. B. van der Meer, *The Bronze Liver of Piacenza* (Amsterdam: J. C. Gieben, 1987).

16. See Benno Landsberger and Hayim Tadmor, "Fragments of Clay Liver Models from Hazor," *Israel Exploration Journal* 14 (1964): 201–18.

17. On this distinction, see Struck, *Birth of the Symbol*, 166–70.

18. See Johnston, *Ancient Greek Divination*, 4–32.

19. Fritz Graf makes a careful effort to distinguish magical and divination traditions while showing how one can serve the other. An important example is the practice of gazing into a liquid. See Fritz Graf, "Magic and Divination," in *The World of Ancient Magic*, ed. David Jordan, Hugo Montgomery, and Einar Thomassen (Bergen: Norwegian Institute at Athens, 1999), 283–98.

20. Struck, *Birth of the Symbol*, 188–89, quoting Cicero, *De divinatione* 1.118.

21. Cicero, *De divinatione* 1.51; translation by W. A. Falconer, *De senectute, De amicitia, De divinatione* (Cambridge, MA: Harvard University Press; London: Heinemann, 1979).

22. For a good survey of divination in rabbinic and cognate literatures, including critical notes on the manuscripts in rabbinic sources, see Yuval Harari, *Ha-Kishuf ha-Yehudi ha-Qadum: Meḥqar, Shitah, Meqorot* (Jerusalem: Mosad Bialik and Yad Ben Zvi, 2010), 313–52.

23. See Baruch A. Levine, *The JPS Torah Commentary: Leviticus* (Philadelphia: Jewish Publication Society, 1989), 133 and 208–9, nn. 32–34; Jeffers, *Magic and Divination* 74–78; and Cryer, *Divination in Ancient Israel*, 284–86.

24. For an overview, see Jeffers, *Magic and Divination*, 144–229.

25. J. C. Greenfield and M. Sokoloff, "An Astrological Text from Qumran (4Q318) and Reflections on Some Zodiacal Names," *Revue de Qumran* 16 (1995): 507–25. See also Michael O. Wise, *Thunder in Gemini and Other Essays on the History, Language and Literature of Second Temple Palestine* (Sheffield: JSOT Press, 1994), 13–60; and Mark J. Geller, "New Documents from the Dead Sea: Babylonian Science in Aramaic," in *Boundaries of the Ancient Near Eastern World: A Tribute to Cyrus H. Gordon*, ed. M. Lubetski, C. Gottlieb, and S. Keller (Sheffield: Sheffield Academic Press, 1998), 224–29.

26. See Philip S. Alexander, "Physiognomy, Initiation, and Rank in the Qumran Community," in *Geschichte-Tradition-Reflexion: Festschrift für Martin Hengel zum 70. Geburtstag*, ed. Hubert Cancik, Hermann Lichtenberger, and Peter Schäfer (Tubingen: Mohr, 1996(, 385–94. See also Ithamar Gruenwald, *Apocalyptic and Merkavah Mysticism* (Leiden:

Brill, 1980), 218–24; and Mladen Popovic, *Reading the Human Body: Physiognomics and Astrology in the Dead Sea Scrolls and Hellenistic-Early Roman Period Judaism* (Leiden: Brill, 2007).

27. J. C. Greenfield and M. Sokoloff, "Astrological and Related Omen Texts in Jewish Palestinian Aramaic," *Journal of Near Eastern Studies* 48 (1989): 201–14; also published in Michael Sokoloff and Joseph Yahalom, *Shirat Bene Ma'arava: Shirim Aramiyim shel Yehude Ereṣ-Yisra'el ba-Tequfah ha-Bizantit* (Jerusalem: Israel Academy of Sciences and the Humanities, 1999), 223–29.

28. A euphemism for the Jews.

29. Greenfield and Sokoloff, "Omen Texts," lines 11–12 (Sokoloff and Yahalom, *Shirat Bene Ma'arava*, text 36, pp. 226–27, lines 41–48). Greenfield and Sokoloff's translation is quoted here. The ellipsis represents the word *šp'*, "abundance," which is unclear in this context; perhaps it means "abundantly white like snow."

30. For Judaism in the Hellenistic and Roman periods, see James H Charlesworth, "Jewish Interest in Astrology during the Hellenistic and Roman Periods," in *Aufstieg und Niedergang der römischen Welt* II.20.2 (1987): 926–49; and Lester J. Ness, "Astrology and Judaism in Late Antiquity" (PhD diss., Miami University, 1990). For the Middle Ages, see Dov Schwartz, *Studies on Astral Magic in Medieval Jewish Thought* (Leiden: Brill-Styx, 2005).

31. See James H. Charlesworth, "The Treatise of Shem," in *The Old Testament Pseudepigrapha*, 1:473–86; and Scott Carroll, "A Preliminary Analysis of the Epistle of Rehoboam," *Journal for the Study of the Pseudepigrapha* 4 (1989): 91–103. Cf. MS TS K1.149 fols. 2a–2b, in Peter Schäfer and Shaul Shaked, *Magische Texte aus der Kairoer Geniza* (Tubingen: Mohr, 1999), 3:274–76, 280–84.

32. For sources, see Saul Lieberman, *Greek in Jewish Palestine* (New York: Jewish Theological Seminary, 1942), 99–100; Charlesworth, "Jewish Interest in Astrology," 930–32; and Alexander Altmann, "Astrology," *Encyclopaedia Judaica*, ed. Fred Skolnik (Detroit: Macmillan, 2007), 2:616–20.

33. There has been much discussion about the significance of these finds. For overviews, see Steven Fine, *Art and Judaism in the Greco-Roman World: Toward a New Jewish Archaeology* (Cambridge: Cambridge University Press, 2005), 196–205; and Rachel Hachlili, "The Zodiac in Ancient Jewish Synagogal Art: A Review," *Jewish Studies Quarterly* 9 (2002): 219–58.

34. See Joseph Yahalom, *Piyyut u-Meṣi'ut ba-Zeman ha-'Atiq* (Tel Aviv: Hakibbutz Hameuchad,), 20–24.

35. On these, see especially Patricia Cox Miller, *Dreams in Late Antiquity: Studies in the Imagination of a Culture* (Princeton, NJ: Princeton University Press, 1994).

36. See, for example, MS TS K1.28 fol. 1a line 11–1b line 7 and 1b lines 8–16, in Peter Schäfer and Shaul Shaked, *Magische Texte aus der Kairoer Geniza* (Tubingen: Mohr, 1994), 1:136; and Peter Schäfer, *Synopse zur Hekhalot-Literatur* (Tubingen: Mohr, 1981), §502 and §613; on this phenomenon, see Michael D. Swartz, *Scholastic Magic*, 47–50; and R. J. Zwi Werblowsky, *Joseph Karo: Lawyer and Mystic* (Oxford: Oxford University Press, 1962), 38–50.

37. B. Ber. 57b; see also Genesis Rabbah 17:5, ed. Theodor and Albeck, 156–57.

38. B. Bava Batra 12b.

39. *Sifra Qedoshim* 6.

40.See Tosefta Shabbat chaps. 6 and 7, ed. Lieberman, 3:22–29.

41. Saul Lieberman, *Tosefta Kifshutah* (New York: Jewish Theological Seminary 1962), 3:79–105; Giuseppe Veltri, *Magie und Halakha* (Tubingen: Mohr, 1997); and Giuseppe Veltri, "The Rabbis and Pliny the Elder: Jewish and Greco-Roman Attitudes toward Magic and Empirical Knowledge," *Poetics Today* 19 (1998): 63–89.

42. Yitzhak Avishor, "'*Darkhe ha-Emori:*' *Ha-Reqaʻ ha-Kenaʻani-Bavli ve-ha-Mivneh ha-Sifruti,*" in *Sefer Meir Valenshtain: Meḥqarim be-Miqra u-ve-Lashon* (Jerusalem: ha-Ḥevrah le-ḥeqer ha-Miqra be-Yisraʼel, 1979), 17–47.

43. Jonathan Seidel, "Charming Criminals: Classification of Magic in the Babylonian Talmud," in *Ancient Magic and Ritual Power*, ed. Marvin W. Meyer and Paul Mirecki (Leiden: Brill, 1995), 161.

44. Tos. Shab. 7:13–14; cf. *Sifre ʻal Sefer Devarim* ed. Finkelstein, 218.

45. B. Ḥullin 95b.

46. For a summary of opinions, see Louis I. Rabbinowitz, "Divination," *Encyclopaedia Judaica*, ed. Fred Skolnik (Detroit: Macmillan, 2007), 6:116. Indeed, the range of opinion in medieval sources regarding that question is an indication of the degree of acceptance such techniques enjoyed in the Middle Ages. On this point, see Harari, *Ha-Kishuf ha-Yehudi*, 313–14.

47. See also b. Gitt. 56a; b. Gitt. 68a; and b. Hag. 15a, where the message, that there is no repentance for Elisha ben Abuya, is confirmed thirteen times. On these stories, see Harari, *Ha-Kishuf*, 318–19.

48. Samuel Daiches, *Babylonian Oil Magic in the Talmud and in the Later Jewish Literature* (London: Jews College, 1913); see also Joseph Dan, "'*Sare Kos ve-Sare Bohen,*'" *Tarbṣ* 32 (1963): 359–69.

49. Sarah Iles Johnston, "Charming Children: The Use of the Child in Ancient Divination," *Arethusa* 34 (2001): 97–117.

50. B. Ber. 55a.

51. Y. Maʻas. S. 4:11 (54b–c); b. Ber. 55a–57a.

52. See, for example, Philip S. Alexander, "Bavli Berakhot 55a–57b: The Talmudic Dreambook in Context," *Journal of Jewish Studies* 46 (1995): 230–48; Ken Frieden, *Freud's Dream of Interpretation* (Albany: SUNY Press, 1990), 73–93; Richard Kalmin, *Sages, Stories, Authors, and Editors in Rabbinic Babylonia* (Atlanta: Scholars Press, 1994), 61–85; and Maren Niehoff, "A Dream Which Is Not Interpreted Is like a Letter Which Is Not Read," *Journal of Jewish Studies* 43 (1992): 58–84.

53. On this idea see Frieden, *Freud's Dream of Interpretation*.

54. Galit Hasan-Rokem, "Communication with the Dead in Jewish Dream Culture," in *Dream Cultures: Explorations in the Comparative History of Dreaming*, ed. David Shulman and Guy G. Stroumsa (New York: Oxford University Press, 1999), 212.

55. See especially T. Maʻas. S. 5:9.

56. That question is debated in b. Ber. 18a–19a.

57. Avot de-Rabbi Natan A, in *Aspects of Rabbinic Theology*, ed. Solomon Schechter, 2nd ed. (New York: Schocken Books, 1961), chap. 3, pp. 16–17).

58. B. BB 134a and b. Suk. 28a. On the entire passage, see David J. Halperin, *The Merkavah in Rabbinic Literature* (New Haven, CT: American Oriental Society, 1980), 137–38; cf. David J. Halperin, "The Ibn Sayyad Traditions, and the Legend of al-Dajjal," *Journal of the American Oriental Society* 96 (1976): 219–20.

59. Cf., for example, Cant. 5:2.

60. B. Gittin 45a.

61. On the raven's ability to predict the future, see Ginzberg, *Legends* 5:185, n. 46, citing Philo, *Questions in Genesis* 2.35; cf. Tos. Shab. 7:13–14, discussed earlier. See also the sources cited there on the raven's rebellious nature, especially b. Sanh. 108b; see also chap. 5, n. 72.

62. B. Sanh. 101a.

63. Daiches, *Babylonian Oil Magic*, 18–19.

64. Cf. I. Tzvi Abusch, "*Alaktu* and *Halakhah*: Oracular Decision, Divine Revelation," *Harvard Theological Review* 80 (1987): 20.

65. See Jacob Neusner, "Rabbi and Magus in Third-Century Sasanian Babylonia," *History of Religions* 6 (1966): 169–78.

66. See Israel Friedlaender, "A Mohammedan Book on Augury in Hebrew Characters," *Jewish Quarterly Review* 19 (1907): 84–103.

67. See Gershom Scholem, "*Hakarat Panim ve-Sidre Sirtutin*," in *Sefer Asaf: Qoveṣ Ma`amare Meḥqar Musag li-khvod ha-Rav Professor Simḥah Asaf*, ed. Umberto Cassuto, Joseph Klausner, and Joshua Gutman (Jerusalem: Mosad ha-Rav Kook, 1952–53), 459–95; and Peter Schäfer, *Geniza-Fragmente zur Hekhalot-Literatur* (Tubingen: Mohr, 1984), 135–39 (=G12).

68. Esther-Miriam Wagner and Gideon Bohak, "T-S AS 157.50: A Twitch Divination Text in the Hand of Ḥalfon b. Manasseh," Cambridge University Library Taylor-Schechter Research Unit Fragment of the Month, April 2008. Available at http://www.lib.cam.ac.uk/ Taylor-Schechter/fotm/april-2008/.

69. Ibid., referring to MS TS NS 33.130.

70. See, for example, Meir Backal, *Goralot Urim ve-Tumim he-Ḥadash ve-ha-shalem 'im Pitron ha-She'elot* (Jerusalem: Backal, 1995); Meir Backal, *Ḥokhmat ha-Partsuf ha-Shalem* (Jerusalem, 1996–97).

71. Michael D. Swartz, "Book and Tradition in Hekhalot and Magical Literatures," *Journal of Jewish Thought and Philosophy* 3 (1994): 189–229, in which I describe these introductions as alternative chains of tradition authorizing and promoting the book for the reader; see also Michael D. Swartz, "Chains of Tradition in the Avodah Piyyutim," in *Judaism, Christianity, and the Roman Empire*, ed. Natalie Dohrman and Annette Yoshiko Reed (Philadelphia: University of Pennsylvania Press, forthcoming), and the sources cited there.

72. Michael Meerson, "Book Is a Territory: A Hebrew Book of Fortune in Context," *Jewish Studies Quarterly* 13 (2006): 388–411.

73. Cf. Emilie Savage-Smith and Marion B. Smith, *Islamic Geomancy and a Thirteenth-Century Divinatory Device* (Malibu, CA: Undena, 1980). My thanks to Ms. Okun for her advice regarding this subject.

74. Martin S. Cohen, *Catalog of Practical Cabala Manuscripts in the Library of the Jewish Theological Seminary* (New York, 1983).

75. M. Yoma 2:1.

76. That is, the community.

77. Ps. 116:13–14. For the Hebrew text and notes, see Michael D. Swartz, "*Pulhan ha-Miqdash be-Sifrut ha-Magiah ha-Yehudit*," Pe'amim, the Quarterly of the Ben Zvi Institute 85 (2000): 67.

78. See Michael D. Swartz, "Sacrificial Themes in Jewish Magic," in *Ancient Magic and Ritual Power*, ed. Marvin Meyer and Paul Mirecki (Leiden: Brill, 2002), 2:303–15; and Swartz, "*Pulḥan ha-Miqdash*." We can also see this in a magic *Sotah* ritual published originally by A. Marmorstein and most recently by Guiseppi Veltri, Peter Schäfer, and Shaul Shaked, in which the synagogue substitutes for the Temple and the magician substitutes for the priest. See Schäfer and Shaked, *Magische Texte aus der Kairoer Geniza* 1:17–45.

CHAPTER 5

1. Bezalel Bar-Kochva, *Pseudo-Hecataeus, On the Jews: Legitimizing the Jewish Diaspora* (Berkeley: University of California Press, 1996), 49–53, translating *Josephus Apion* 1.201–4.

2. Num. 17:32.

3. Num. 21:16–18.

4. A hard stone or worm that, according to legend, was used to hew the stone of Solomon's Temple. See Louis Ginzberg, *Legends of the Jews* (Philadelphia: Jewish Publication Society, 1947), 5:53; and Michael Sokoloff, *A Dictionary of Jewish Palestinian Aramaic* (Ramat Gan: Bar Ilan University Press, 1990), s.v. *shamir*.

5. Gen. 22:13.

6. On parallels, see chap. 2, n. 2.

7. See Genesis Rabbah 1:10, ed. Theodor and Albeck, 9; and Ginzberg, *Legends of the Jews*, 5:5–6, n. 10.

8. Cf. M. Shabbat 7:2, which lists the so-called fathers of labor, the thirty-nine classes of work prohibited on the Sabbath, which, although it is not comprehensive in legal terms, does constitute a step-by-step account of the actions that comprise civilization. See Robert Goldenberg, "Law and Spirit in Talmudic Religion," in *Jewish Spirituality from the Bible to the Middle Ages*, ed. Arthur A. Green (New York: Crossroads,1987), 232–52; Sidney Hoenig, "The Designated Number of Kinds of Labor Prohibited on the Sabbath," *Jewish Quarterly Review* 68 (1978): 193–208; Yitzhak D. Gilat, "'*Al L'T Avot Mal'akhot Shabbat*," *Tarbis* 48 (1979): 222–28; and Michael D. Swartz, "Scholasticism as a Comparative Category and the Study of Judaism," in *Scholasticism: Cross-Cultural and Comparative Perspectives*, ed. José I. Cabezón (Albany: SUNY Press, 1998), 96–97.

9. Robert Parker, *Miasma: Pollution and Purification in Early Greek Religion* (Oxford: Clarendon Press, 1983).

10. Ibid., 123.

11. Ibid., 121.

12. Lev. 3:17, 7:26, 17:10–14; Deut. 12:15–16, 20–24.

13. Genesis Rabbah 22.9, ed. Theodor and Albeck, 216; see the commentary there, which argues that this midrash is directed to the Mishnah's exegesis.

14. See Ginzberg, *Legends* 5:140, n. 21.

15. Lines 357–58; see Michael D. Swartz and Joseph Yahalom, *Avodah: Ancient Poems for Yom Kippur* (University Park: Pennsylvania State University Press, 2005), 104.

16. That is, the earth.

17. Abel's blood.

18. *Mekhilta, Beshallaḥ* chap. 9, ed. Horovitz and Rabin, p. 145; cf. also Targum Pseudo-Jonathan and the Yerushalmi Targum to Exod. 15:12.

19. Cf. also *Pirqe de-Rabbi Eliezer* chap. 42.

20. Y. Taan. 4:6 (69a–b); *Pesiqta de-Rav Kahana*, 2nd ed., *Ekhah* 7, ed. Mandelbaum, vol. 1, 258–59; b. Git 57b; b. Sanh. 96b; Lamentations Rabbah 4:13, ed. S. Buber, *Ekhah Rabbah* (Vilna, 1899), 149; the version in proem 23, *Ekhah Rabbah,* ed. Buber, pp. 21–22, is copied from the Babylonian Talmud; see Buber's commentary; the version in Ecclesiastes Rabbah is, in turn, taken from Lamentations Rabbah proem 23. On this complex of stories, see Sheldon H. Blank, "The Death of Zechariah in Rabbinic Literature," *Hebrew Union College Annual* 12/13 (1937–38): 327–46; Ginzberg, *Legends of the Jews* 6: 396–97; Betsey Halpern Amaru, "The Killing of the Prophets: Unraveling a Midrash," *Hebrew Union College Annual* 54 (1983): 153–80; Galit Hasan-Rokem, *Web of Life: Folklore and Midrash in Rabbinic Literature* (Stanford, CA: Stanford University Press, 2000), 169–71; Yaron Z. Eliav, *God's Mountain: The Temple Mount in Time, Place, and Memory* (Baltimore: Johns Hopkins University Press, 2005), 78; Ra'anan Boustan, *From Martyr to Mystic: The Story of the Ten Martyrs, Hekhalot Rabbati, and the Making of Merkavah Mysticism* (Tubingen: Mohr, 2005), 166, n. 66; and Richard Kalmin, "Zechariah and the Bubbling Blood: An Ancient Tradition in Jewish, Christian, and Muslim Literature," in *Jews and Christians in Sasanian Babylonia,* ed. Geoffrey Herman (Piscataway, NJ: Gorgias Press, forthcoming). My thanks to Professor Kalmin for making a copy of his article available to me in advance of publication.

21. Matthew 23:34–35 and Luke 11:50 draw a connection between the innocent blood of Abel and the blood of Zechariah (there conflated with the Zechariah ben Berachiah of the prophetic book) but do not reflect directly on the belief in the agency of blood. On this passage, see John Chapman, "Zecharias, Slain between the Temple and the Altar," *Journal of Theological Studies* 13 (1911–12): 398–410. In 333 CE, the Bourdeaux Pilgrim was shown the blood of Zechariah on the Temple Mount; by that time the Zechariah of 2 Chronicles 24 had become confused with Zecharias the father of John the Baptist. See John Wilkinson, *Egeria's Travels,* 3rd ed. (Warminster: Aris & Phillip, 1999), 30. On the issue of the identity of Zechariah in this story, see also Kalmin, "Zechariah and the Bubbling Blood."

22. See Roger W. Cowley, "The 'Blood of Zechariah' (MT 23:35) in Ethiopian Exegetical Tradition," in *Studia Patristica 18: Papers of the Ninth International Conference on Patristic Studies 1983* 1 (1986): 293–302; and Kalmin, "Zechariah and the Bubbling Blood."

23. On the significance of these shifts in language, see Cowley, "The 'Blood of Zechariah,'" and Kalmin, "Zechariah and the Bubbling Blood."

24. That is, Zechariah was all three.

25. In Lamentations Rabbah 4:13, this statement follows the story of the blood of Zechariah.

26. See 2 Kings 25:8–10.

27. The words in square brackets, which appear in the parallels in Palestinian midrashim, were added to the Leiden manuscript by a scribe. In those parallels, the second occurrence of the phrase "they said to him" is absent, making both sentences part of the people's statement to Nebuzaradan.

28. In the parallels to this version of the story in Lamentations Rabbah 4:13 (early fifth century CE) and *Pesiqta de-Rav Kahanah* (late fifth or early sixth century CE), the blood of the victims boiled and accumulated until it reached the tomb of Zechariah, presumably the tomb known as such in the valley of Kidron. See *Pesiqta de-Rav Kahanah* Ekhah 7, ed. Mandelbaum, 259, which adds a scriptural prooftext in Hosea 4:2: "They break all bounds, and blood touches blood."

29. Matthew 23:35 states that he was killed "between the sanctuary and the altar"; cf. Luke 11:51; on these passages see Chapman, "Zecharias."

30. See Tosefta Kippurim 1:12, ed. Lieberman, 3:224–35, in which a passage condemns the priesthood of the Second Temple period for its corruption by telling a story in which a young man is stabbed on the ramp to the altar. The priests worry about whether the bloody knife has caused impurity to the inner hall or the courtyard. The Tosefta comments that "the purity of the knife was more important to them than the spilling of blood."

31. B. Sanh. 96b.

32. In the Palestinian versions, he places the Jerusalemites on the gallows. In the Babylonian version (b. Gittin 57b and b. Sanh. 96b), he threatens to tear their flesh with iron combs.

33. In the Babylonian version, he slaughters the great and lesser courts (Sanhedrin), young men and women, and schoolchildren.

34. The story is ambiguous in this version. In the Babylonian Talmud's version, Nebuzaradan calls out to Zechariah by name.

35. George Alexander Kohut, "Blood Test as Proof of Kinship in Jewish Folklore," *Journal of the American Oriental Society* 24 (1903): 129–44; Tamar Alexander-Frizer, *The Pious Sinner: Ethics and Aesthetics in the Medieval Hasidic Narrative* (Tubingen: Mohr, 1991), 39–52. These studies relate a medieval story in which the blood of a son proves his kinship with his father to motif H486.1, in Stith Thompson, *Motif-Index of Folk-Literature; A Classification of Narrative Elements in Folktales, Ballads, Myths, Fables, Mediaeval Romances, Exempla, Fabliaux, Jest-Books, and Local Legends* (Bloomington: Indiana University Press, 1955–58).

36. In Lamentations Rabbah 4:13, God also signals to the blood to boil when Nebuzaradan first enters the Temple Mount.

37. Blank, "The Death of Zechariah," 340, n. 23, suggests that this tendency to look on Nebuzaradan more favorably may be explained by how he is portrayed in Jer. 40:2–4.

38. Kalmin, "Zechariah and the Bubbling Blood."

39. On the role of animals in myth, see especially Sarah Isles Johnston, "A New Web for Arachne," in *Antike Mythen: Medien, Transformationen und Konstruktionen*, ed. Christine Walde and Ueli Dill (Berlin: de Gruyter, 2009), 1–22.

40. Victor Aptowitzer, "The Rewarding and Punishing of Animals and Inanimate Objects: On the Aggadic View of the World," *Hebrew Union College Annual* 3 (1926): 117–55. On medieval treatments of this motif, see Eric Lawee, "The Sins of the Fauna in Midrash, Rashi, and Their Medieval Interlocutors," *Jewish Studies Quarterly* 17 (2010): 56–98.

41. See Ginzberg, *Legends of the Jews*, 1:23–24 and 5:34–36.

42. See ibid., 3:82–85 and 6:31–32.

43. Victor Aptowitzer, "Die Anteilnahme der physischen Welt an der Schicksalen des Menschen," *Monatsschrift für Geschichte und Wissenschaft des Judentums* 28 (1920): 227–31, 305–13; and 29 (1921): 71–87, 164–87.

44. Leviticus Rabbah 22:3, ed., Margulies, 499–502; see also Margulies's notes for further parallels and variants); *Avot de-Rabbi Natan*, ed. Schechter, version B, chap. 7, 20–21; b. Gittin 56b; *Pirqe de-Rabbi Eliezer* 49.

45. Galit Hasan-Rokem, "Within Limits and Beyond: History and Body in Midrashic Texts," *International Folklore Review* 9 (1993): 5–12; Galit Hasan-Rokem, "Narratives in Dialogue: A Folk Literary Perspective on Interreligious Contacts in the Holy Land in Rabbinic Literature of Late Antiquity," in *Sharing the Sacred; Religious Contacts and Conflicts in the Holy Land, First-Fifteenth Centuries CE*, ed. Arieh Kofsky and Guy G. Stroumsa (Jerusalem: Yad Izhak Ben Zvi, 1998), 109–29. See also Joshua Levinson, "'Tragedies Naturally Performed': Fatal Charades, Parodia Sacra, and the Death of Titus," in *Jewish Culture and Society under the Christian Roman Empire*, ed. Seth Schwartz and Richard Kalmin (Lueven: Peeters, 2003), 349–82.

46. Hasan-Rokem, "Within Limits," 10.

47. Leviticus Rabbah 22:2, ed. Margulies, 498.

48. New Jewish Publication Society (NJPS) translates the first part of this verse as "Thus the greatest advantage of the earth is his."

49. Following Sokoloff's emendation in Sokoloff, *Dictionary*, s.v. *nsk*. Margulies, *Vayiqra Rabbah*, 498, suggests *swgy' lmswk gpn'*, "fences to enclose vines."

50. Leviticus Rabbah 22:1, ed. Margulies, 494–95.

51. Leviticus Rabbah 22:2, ed. Margulies, 498.

52. Leviticus Rabbah 22:3, ed. Margulies, 499.

53. Hasan-Rokem, "Within Limits," 7, comments that the Aramaic gloss about the whether it was the blood of the sacrificial goats or the Holy of Holies takes the form of a rumor and heightens the ambiguity of the sexual connotations of the image.

54. This statement takes the form of a proverb in Aramaic.

55. Hasan-Rokem, "Within Limits," 8.

56. The verb used here is *ramaz*, the same verb that is used in the earlier story of the blood of Zechariah.

57. Heb., *nyqyty' brbryh*, transliterating Gk νικητής βαρβάρων. Hasan-Rokem, "Within Limits," 9, notes the use of Greek words here to highlight the foreignness of the setting of the emperor's triumph.

58. Heb. *dyplwpwtwryn*; transliterating Gk διπλοποτήριον.

59. This is Titus speaking, referring to himself.

60. As Hasan-Rokem, "Within Limits," 9, observes, "Validation by actual witnesses often appears at the end of narratives in the legend genre to connect it with historical reality."

61. Hasan-Rokem, "Within Limits."

62. In Leviticus Rabbah 22:4, ed. Margulies, 503–11, there are nine such stories. In Genesis Rabbah 10:7, ed. Theodor and Albeck, 79–83, the first five of these appear, with minor variations, introduced as in Leviticus Rabbah by the point that God does his will by means of the smallest of creatures. In Tanḥuma Buber Ḥuqat 1, 98–99, six of the nine appear. In the two latter versions, the Titus story follows the other stories. See also Numbers Rabbah 18:22.

63. Eli Yassif, *The Hebrew Folktale: History, Genre, Meaning* (Bloomington: Indiana University Press, 1999), 238.

64. Leviticus Rabbah 22:4, ed. Margulies, 503–4.

65. Tanh. Buber Ḥuqat 1, 98. This version is written in Hebrew, whereas Leviticus Rabbah's version is in Aramaic.

66. K952.1 in Thompson, *Motif-Index* 4: 355.

67. Or, perhaps, hissing.

68. Leviticus Rabbah 22:4, ed. Margulies, 505.

69. Lit., "walking about." According to Sokoloff, *Dictionary*, s.v. *ṭyyl*, a euphemism for defecating; cf. Margulies's commentary.

70. Leviticus Rabbah 22:4, ed. Margulies, 505.

71. Ibid.

72. B. Gittin 45a, on which see the previous chapter. For another example of the raven's unattractive habits, see Leviticus Rabbah 19.1, ed. Margulies, 415.

73. See Bar Kochva *Pseudo-Hecataeus*, 57–70.

74. On *telos* in rabbinic anthropology, see Jonathan Wyn Schofer, "Self, Subject, and Chosen Subjection: Rabbinic Ethics and Comparative Possibilities," *Journal of Religious Ethics* 33 (2005): 255–91.

CHAPTER 6

1. Smith, "Sacred Persistence."

2. Abusch, "*Alaktu* and *Halakhah*."

3. Ibid., 34.

4. Cox Miller, *The Corporeal Imagination*, 31.

5. Ibid.

6. Ibid., 32.

7. See Polymnia Athanassiadi, "Dreams, Theurgy and Freelance Divination: The Testimony of Iamblichus," *Journal of Roman Studies* 83 (1993): 115–30.

8. See Sarah Isles Johnston, "Animating Statues: A Case Study in Ritual," *Arethusa* 41 (2008): 445–77.

Index

Aaron, 39, 43. *See also* High Priest
Abusch, Zvi, 11, 92
Abraham, 39, 41, 65
Adam, 26, 40–42
Agency, 75, 80, 83, 89, 90
Angels, 50, 51–52, 59, 62, 68, 80, 105n79
Animals, 8, 60, 84–89, 96n11, 103n40; created for human consumption, 30–32, 101n79; myths about, 84; punishment of, 84
Art, 10, 39
"Atah Konanta Olam Me-Rosh," 52
Astrology, 59, 63
Austin, J. L., 1
Automatic writing, 57
Avodah, 8, 25–32, 48–52. *See also individual piyyutim*
Avot (Mishnah Tractate), 13, 42, 76, 98n9
Avot de-Rabbi Natan, 19–20
"Az be-En Kol," ("When All Was Not"), 25, 28–29, 48, 49, 50, 52, 78
"Azkir Gevurot Elohah" ("Let Me Recount the Wonders of God"), 25–26, 48, 49

Backal, Meir, 70
Barthes, Roland, 34–35
Behemoth, 30
Bell, Catherine, 33
Ben Sira (Ecclesiasticus), 45, 50, 51–52
Benjamin, Walter, 57–58
Bibliomancy, 66
Birds, 65, 68–69, 75. *See also* Raven
Blood, 77–83, 113n28; earth's acceptance of, 78–80; in Greek religion, 77; in Jewish law, 77; sacrificial, 77, 82
Bourdieu, Pierre, 33

Boyarin, Daniel, 96n20, 98n11
Brontology, 62
Brüll, Jacob, 3–5, 7–8

Cage, John, 55–56, 58
Cain and Abel, 77–79
Chance, 55–58, 72–73
Children, 64, 57, 66–67
Chiromancy, 69
Christianity, 6, 36, 93, 95n1
Cicero, 6, 60–61, 68
Clooney, Francis X., 3
Clothing, significance of, 33–35, 53; instrumental and representational functions, 35, 48–50, 53–54
Coon, Lynda L., 36
Creation and Precreation: creation for cultic purpose, 26–27; lists of precreated things, 13, 16–24, 76; lists of things created before Sabbath, 13, 76; myths of Creation, 13–15

Day of Atonement. *See* Yom Kippur
Dead Sea Scrolls, 59, 61
Derrida, Jaques, 6, 96n20
Dietary Laws. *See* Kashrut
Dada, 56–58, 60
Daiches, Samuel, 67, 68
Derrida, Jacques, 6, 96
Divination, 8, 40, 44, 75, 89–90; Arabic divination texts, 69–70; in Bible, 61, 65; books of, 69–72; in the Greco-Roman world, 60–61, 67, 89–90; as hermeneutics, 6, 11, 59, 92; in Mesopotamia, 59, 62; oil divination, 67, 68; in rabbinic literature, 64–69; in statecraft and established institutions, 6, 62

Dreams, 57, 59, 61, 63–64, 67–68
Dura-Europas, 39

Eilberg-Schwartz, Howard, 11
"Emet Mah Nehedar," ("Truly How Glorious"), 51
Esau, 41–42, 103n40

Fashion, 34–35
Faur, José, 5–6
Feldman, Morton, 55–56
Fischel, Henry, 42
Fishbane, Michael, 6, 13
Flood, 28
Food, 29–31
Frog and scorpion, 87–88

Garden of Eden, 17, 18, 19, 23, 40–42
Gates, Henry Louis, 9
Genesis Rabbah (*Bereshit Rabbah*), 15–16, 20–21, 24, 41, 78
Genizah, 62–64, 69–72
Geomancy, 71
Ginzberg, Louis, 97n4, 98n13
Goralot, 70–72
Graf, Fritz, 107n19

Handelman, Susan, 6
Harari, Yuval, 107n22
Hasan-Rokem, Galit, 68, 84, 87
Hecataeus, 75
Herod, 35
High Priest: glorification of, 48–50; as symbol or representative of Israel, 40, 45–47. *See also* Vestments
Humankind, creation of, 26–27

Iamblichus, 6, 93
Isaac, 41, 65
Ibn Ezra, Abraham, 70
Islam 1, 19,
Israel, 20; land of, 21–22

Jacob, 41–42, 49, 63
Jews, as "people of the book," 1; in omen literature, 63. *See also* Israel

Jonah, 87
Jonathan, 4, 65
Joseph, 46, 49, 63, 104n58
Josephus, 35, 39, 44, 75

Kabbalah, 13
Kalmin, Richard, 83
Kashrut, 19–20, 31, 96n11
Kraeling, Carl, 39

Leichtz, Eric, 59
Letter of Aristeas, 39
Leviathan, 30, 100n70
Levine, Moshe, 35
Leviticus Rabbah (*Vayiqra Rabbah*), 46, 87–89
Lieberman, Saul, 6, 59
Liebes, Yehudah, 13
Logocentrism, 6, 7
Logos, 15–16, 98n11
Lots. *See* Goralot

Magic, 1, 10, 40, 60, 107n19, 111n78
Manetti, Giovanni, 59
Mekhilta de-Millu'im, 42–44, 103n41
Mekhilta de-Rabbi Ishmael, 78
Memorization, 3, 7, 96n10
Merkavah mysticism. *See* Mysticism, early Jewish
Mesopotamia: vestments in, 35–36; divination traditions, 59, 62
Messiah, 18–20, 23
Messianic era. *See* World to come
Midrash, 8, 9, 13, 40, 59, 92, 94. *See also individual midrashim*
Midrash to Psalms, 17–19
Mishnah, 10, 13, 37, 46, 111n13
Miller, Patricia Cox, 6, 93
Moses, 36, 43
Mosquito, 84–87
Mysticism, 13; early Jewish, 50, 62, 105n79
Myth, definitions of, 13–14

Neusner, Jacob, 101n10
Nebuzaradan, 80–83
Necromancy, 60–61, 68

Noah, 41, 68

Oppenheim, A. Leo, 35–36,

Palmomancy, 70
Pantextuality, 6, 7, 27, 94, 97n39
Parker, Robert, 77
Patriarchs, 18–21
Pesiqta de-Rav Kahana, 80
Philo, 44–45, 52, 98n11
Physiognomy, 62, 69–70
Piyyut, 8, 10, 63, 92. See also Avodah
Platonism, 93
Proclus, 93
Proverbs, Book of, 14–15
Pseudo-Philo, 39

Rabbinic Judaism, 5–7, 9–11, 13–16, 93–94
Randomness, 55–57, 60
Raven, 29, 68–69, 110n61, 115n72
Repentance, 18, 20
Ritual, 2–3, 24, 27, 33, 54; language, 1; discourse, 33–34
Robe, 38
Rubens, Alfred, 38

Sabbath, 22, 42, 76, 81, 111n8
Sacrifice, 8, 25, 27, 32, 34–35, 47, 82, 93
Sayings of the Fathers. See Avot
Scholem, Gershom, 13, 70
Seder Eliyahu Rabbah, 16–19
Semiotics, 2, 36, 53, 57, 73
Sepphoris, 39
Shekhinah, 43–44
Sifra, 65. See also Mekhilta de-Millu'im
Sifre Deuteronomy, 16–19
Signifying and signification, 7–11, 36–37, 53–54, 72–73, 91–94
Signs and signifiers, 2–5, 7–9; creation of, 27–31, 60
Siman, 3–5, 31, 68. See also Signs and signifiers
Snakes, 88–89
Sorites, 42
Sortes, 70
Surrealism, 56–58

Stern, David, 6
Synagogue poetry. See Piyyut

Tabernacle, 22, 28,
Tanḥuma, 16–19, 22–24, 41–42, 87
Talmud: Babylonian, 16–19, 64–69, 80–83; Palestinian, 46–47, 8–83; Talmudic mnemonics, 7
Teleology, 8, 27, 76–77, 90, 113n30, 115n74
Temple, 48, 71, 93, 111n78; creation of, 13; destruction of, 45, 80
Testament of Levi, 45
Theurgy, 93
Thompson, Stith, 88
Throne of Glory, 19, 20–24
Torah: as blueprint for the world, 14–16, 28, 31–32; precreation of, 14–16, 18, 20–22, 24; as source of meaning, 2, 8, 91
Tosefta, 65

Qur'an, 95n1

Urim and Thumim, 37, 44, 61, 71–72

Vestments: in the Avodah, 48–54; bells, 37, 38, 39, 49–50; in Christianity, 36; components of, 36–40; custody of, 35; in Mesopotamian religion, 35–36; miraculous origin of, 40–44; as model of the Cosmos, 44–45; precious stones in, 37–38, 44, 45; in rabbinic literature, 45–47
Vitellius, 35

"Ways of the Amorites," 65
Weinfield, Moshe, 22
Wisdom, 14–16
Wisdom of Solomon, 15–16, 44–45
World to come, 19, 29–30

Yahalom, Joseph, 28
Yom Kippur, 25, 27, 35, 47, 51, 81, 85–87. See also Avodah
Yose ben Yose, 25, 48, 49, 52

Zechariah ben Jehoiadah, 80–83
Zekhut Avot (Merit of the fathers), 49

About the Author

MICHAEL D. SWARTZ is Professor of Hebrew and Religious Studies in the Department of Near Eastern Languages and Cultures and at the Melton Center for Jewish Studies at Ohio State University. His books include *Scholastic Magic: Ritual and Revelation in Early Jewish Mysticism*; *Mystical Prayer in Ancient Judaism: An Analysis of Ma'aseh Merkavah*; *Avodah: Ancient Poems for Yom Kippur* (with Joseph Yahalom); and *Hebrew and Aramaic Incantation Texts from the Cairo Genizah: Selected Texts from Taylor-Schechter Box K1* (with Lawrence H. Schiffman). He also served as the associate editor for Judaica for the second edition of the *Encyclopedia of Religion*.